Men-at-Arms • 553

The Union Army 1861–65 (1)

The Regular Army and the Territories

Ron Field • Illustrated by Marco Capparoni

Series editors Martin Windrow & Nick Reynolds

OSPREY PUBLISHING
Bloomsbury Publishing Plc
Kemp House, Chawley Park, Cumnor Hill, Oxford OX2 9PH, UK
29 Earlsfort Terrace, Dublin 2, Ireland
1385 Broadway, 5th Floor, New York, NY 10018, USA
E-mail: info@ospreypublishing.com
www.ospreypublishing.com

OSPREY is a trademark of Osprey Publishing Ltd

First published in Great Britain in 2024

A catalog record for this book is available from the British Library.

ISBN: PB 9781472855794; eBook 9781472855763;
ePDF 9781472855770; XML 9781472855787

24 25 26 27 28   10 9 8 7 6 5 4 3 2 1

Index by Rob Munro
Typeset by PDQ Digital Media Solutions, Bungay, UK
Printed and bound in India by Replika Press Private Ltd.

Acknowledgments

The author is very grateful to the following for their help in the production of this
volume: Tom, Jason, Brandon, and Christian Liljenquist for access to their
collection at the Library of Congress, Washington, DC; Kay Peterson, Archives
Center, Smithsonian National Museum of American History, Washington, DC;
Peter Harrington, curator of the Anne S.K. Brown Military Collection, Brown
University, Providence, Rhode Island; Kellen Cutsworth, Photo Services
Specialist, Denver Public Library, Denver, Colorado; David M. Sullivan, Editor,
Company of Military Historians, Washington, DC; Dr. Michael R. Cunningham;
Daniel J. Binder; Don Troiani; Steven and Theresa Karnes; and Brian T. White.

Artist's note

Readers may care to note that the original paintings from which the color plates
in this book were prepared are available for private sale. All reproduction
copyright whatsoever is retained by the publishers. All inquiries should be
addressed to:

marcocapparoni.com

The publishers regret that they can enter into no correspondence upon
this matter.

Title-page illustration: This lithograph produced by Henry A. Ogden in 1885
depicts staff, field, and line officers, plus enlisted men, of the Regular Army for
the period 1858–61. The staff officer at left is distinguished by a dark-blue
ground in his shoulder straps. Standing on the steps, a dragoon lieutenant
colonel or major has orange shoulder straps, and those of the infantry captain at
center are sky blue. A dragoon sergeant with orange lace trim on his jacket and
trousers stands at far right; an infantry private with musket is beyond him. All
have their Pattern 1858 hats looped up on the correct (right) side as per General
Orders No. 4 of February 26, 1861, except for the infantry captain who still has
his hat looped up on the left side as per General Orders No. 3 of March 24,
1858. All wear dark-blue trousers officially prescribed until December 16, 1861.
(Anne S.K. Brown Military Collection)

THE UNION ARMY 1861–65 (1)

THE REGULAR ARMY AND THE TERRITORIES

INTRODUCTION

On the eve of the beginning of the Civil War in April 1861 the total paper strength of the United States Regular Army was 16,402 officers and men, of whom 14,657 were present for duty scattered over a large continent (Eicher & Eicher 2001: 46). Within this number there were four general officers – Winfield Scott as major general, and William S. Harney, David E. Twiggs, and John E. Wool as brigadier generals – plus about 1,104 commissioned officers.

Of these, 361 staff officers were assigned to six departments, two corps, and one bureau, each headed by a colonel. These consisted of the Quartermaster Department, Ordnance Department, Inspector-General's Department, Medical Department, Pay Department, and Subsistence Department; the Corps of Engineers; the Corps of Topographical Engineers; and the Bureau of Military Justice. To these were added the Provost Marshal General's Bureau in May 1863, and the Bureau of Refugees, Freedmen, and Abandoned Lands in March 1865.

Of 743 line officers, 351 served in ten infantry regiments; 210 in four artillery regiments; and 182 in four mounted regiments (Newell 2014: 50). Approximately 13,500 noncommissioned officers (NCOs) and enlisted men were assigned to various branches of foot and mounted service. About 62,000 officers and men served in the Regular Army during the Civil War years (1861–65). By March 31, 1865, however, it consisted of just 21,669 officers and men, of whom only 13,880 were present for duty (Eicher & Eicher 2001: 46).

Of the new branches of service, specialists, and Territories, the United States Colored Troops enrolled 99,337 men, while the United States Indian Home Guard recruited 3,530 men (Eicher & Eicher 2001: 53). A total of about 2,570 men enlisted in the two regiments of United States Sharpshooters (Stevens 1892: 512). The Invalid Corps/Veteran Reserve Corps contained about 60,000 men from 1863 through 1865 (Wagner *et al.* 2002: 441–42). Although the overall size of the Ambulance Corps is not known, by the summer of 1864 that in the Army of the Potomac alone numbered 66 officers and 2,600 men (Ginn 1997: 11–13). The Military Telegraph Service amounted to 1,079 officers and men (Bates 1907: 20). About 2,900 officers and men served in the Signal Corps, albeit not at any one time (Coker & Stokes 1994: 3).

In the Territories a total of 16,871 volunteers were provided to the Union Army as follows: Colorado 4,903; Dakota 206; New Mexico and Arizona 6,561; Nebraska 3,157; Nevada 1,080; and Washington 964 (Eicher & Eicher 2001: 53).

This detail from Plate 172 of the *Atlas to Accompany the Official Records of the Union and Confederate Armies 1861–1865* shows the large "General Service" button worn by Union Army enlisted men. (Author's collection)

This detail from Plate 172 of the *Atlas to Accompany the Official Records of the Union and Confederate Armies 1861–1865* shows the large "General Staff" button worn by Union generals and some General Staff officers. (Author's collection)

GENERAL OFFICERS

Since 1787 the President of the United States had been the Constitutional Commander-in-Chief of the Army and Navy, and of the state militia when called into service. On March 4, 1861, this became the responsibility of President Abraham Lincoln. The ranking officer of the US Army was known as the General-in-Chief with the rank of either major general or lieutenant general. Throughout the Civil War years this role was fulfilled by Winfield Scott (July 5, 1841–November 1, 1861); George B. McClellan (November 1, 1861–March 11, 1862); Henry W. Halleck (July 23, 1862–March 9, 1864); and Ulysses S. Grant (March 9, 1864–March 4, 1869). Abolished during the Revolutionary War (1775–83), the rank of lieutenant general was revived in 1855 when Scott received a brevet promotion to that rank. Both Halleck and McClellan were major generals. In 1864, Grant was appointed lieutenant general when he took command of the Union Army.

With headquarters at Washington, DC, the Quartermaster General in charge of supplies, including clothing and equipage, for the Army until April 22, 1861, was Brigadier General Joseph E. Johnston. Following the outbreak of war, Johnston resigned to enter the Confederate service, and was replaced by Brigadier General Montgomery C. Meigs of the Corps of Engineers, who did not take up the post until June 13, 1861. As a result, Major Ebenezer S. Sibley served as acting chief of the department. Once in place, Meigs proved to be a competent administrator in times of emergency, and remained in post almost continually until 1882.

Since 1858, the dress uniform for generals consisted of a dark-blue Pattern 1851 double-breasted frock coat with a skirt that extended "from two-thirds to three-fourths of the distance from the top of the hip to the bend of the knee"; plain dark-blue trousers; and a Pattern 1858 hat of best black felt (*Regulations* 1861: 3 & 6). Of "General Staff" pattern and bearing a partial representation of the coat of arms of

The chasseur-type cap worn by Major General George B. McClellan was made by Benjamin H. Stinemetz, of 236 Pennsylvania Avenue, Washington, DC. (Smithsonian Institution NMAH, AF.56531)

the United States, the gilt, convex buttons on the coat were arranged in three sets of three for a major general, and four sets of two for a brigadier general. When Grant became a lieutenant general in 1864, the button arrangement remained the same as for a major general. The coat collar and straight cuffs were of dark-blue velvet. On duty, a general officer wore gold bullion epaulets with "dead and bright" gold bullion fringe, ½in. in diameter and 3½in. long. The epaulet straps for a General-in-Chief bore three silver embroidered five-pointed stars in graduated sizes with the largest inside the brass crescent; for major general, two silver embroidered stars with the largest star in the crescent; and for brigadier general, a single star.

Epaulets were replaced by gold-bordered shoulder straps with a black velvet ground bearing the same configuration of embroidered stars when not on duty, and on certain duties off parade, such as Courts of Inquiry and Boards, inspection of barracks and hospitals, work parties and fatigue duties, and upon the march, except when there was an immediate expectation of meeting the enemy, and also when the "cloak coat" was worn. On November 22, 1864, War Department General Orders No. 286 permitted officers to dispense with all rank insignia except for shoulder straps.

First introduced in 1855 with issuance only to the 1st and 2d Cavalry, the Pattern 1858 "Hardee," or "Jeff Davis," dress hat was looped up on the right side by all ranks. When issued to all of the Army in 1858 it was specified via General Orders No. 3 of March 24, 1858, that general

Photographed with his staff and dignitaries at Miner's Hill, Virginia, in March 1862, Major General George B. McClellan (right hand on tree stump) wears a frock coat with a dark-blue velvet low collar and cuffs, regulation button configuration, three-star shoulder straps, buff waist sash with black leather sword belt, plain dark-blue trousers, and tall boots. He holds a forage cap with tall flat top and flat visor, which was popularly known as the "McClellan" or "Chasseur" cap. Brigadier General George W. Morell, who commanded the First Brigade of Porter's Division, Army of the Potomac, stands third from the left. Behind the tree stump is Lieutenant Colonel Albert V. Colburn, who served as Assistant Adjutant General on McClellan's staff. (Library of Congress LC-DIG-ppmsca-34112)

LIEUT. GENERAL

MAJOR GENERAL

BRIGADIER GENERAL

Published in 1895 in the *Atlas to Accompany the Official Records of the Union and Confederate Armies 1861–1865*, these details from Plate 172 by lithographers Julius Bein & Co. of New York, show the top view of epaulets (above) and shoulder straps (below) worn by general officers of the Union Army during the Civil War. (Author's collection)

LIEUT. GENERAL

MAJOR GENERAL.

BRIGADIER GENERAL

officers, staff officers, and officers of all staff corps including engineers, plus officers and men of all mounted regiments, should loop the hat up on the right side. Officers and men of the infantry and the dismounted branch of the artillery were ordered to loop the hat up on the left side. On February 26, 1861, this changed via General Orders No. 4 and all officers were ordered to loop the hat up on the right side, together with mounted enlisted men, with that of enlisted infantrymen only looped up on the left side (Todd 1974: 62–63).

Hence, the Pattern 1858 hat worn by general officers at the outbreak of the Civil War was of best black felt looped up on the right side with an embroidered Pattern 1858 "eagle" insignia on a black velvet ground for all officers via General Orders No. 4, with the brim edged with ½in.-wide black ribbed silk. Trimmings consisted of a gold cord with acorn-shaped ends, three black ostrich feathers on the left side of the crown, and a gold embroidered wreath encircling the silver letters "US" in Old English script at the front. Occasionally, after 1863 officers of all ranks wore the device of their corps or division pinned on the crown of their hat. For optional wear with full dress, a *chapeau de bras*, or cocked hat, with three black ostrich feathers was also authorized for generals and staff officers via General Orders No. 3 (*MG* 3.2, January 15, 1860: 23). Dark-blue forage caps were often worn in the field with the same insignia as for the hat at the front.

A sword belt of red Russian leather had three gold embroidered stripes, and the slings were also embroidered on both sides. The sword belt was fastened by a Pattern 1851 rectangular gilt plate with a silver wreath encircling the coat of arms of the United States with the motto "E PLURIBUS UNUM" (Out of Many, One) in silver letters upon a scroll. The sword authorized was straight, with "gilt hilt, silver grip, brass or steel scabbard" (*Regulations* 1861: 10). In practice this could be either the general and staff officers' Model 1850 or Model 1860 sword. The rank of general was also indicated by a buff silk net waist sash with silk bullion fringe ends, which was to wrap twice around the waist and tie behind the left hip.

In common with all other officers, generals wore a dark-blue "cloak coat," rather than an overcoat, which had five braids of black silk arranged in a knot on each sleeve. On November 25, 1861, all officers were authorized via General Orders No. 102 to wear the enlisted man's mounted overcoat "in time of actual field service." Gauntlets of whitened or buff leather generally replaced gloves during the war years.

When off duty, all officers from general to second lieutenant could wear a more informal plain dark-blue civilian-pattern coat with roll, or turned-down, collar, which bore no insignia other than regulation buttons, plus a buff, white, or dark-blue vest. Also adopted by officers of all ranks was a blouse that varied in pattern. Some wore privately purchased long, double-breasted garments, while others preferred the regulation flannel blouse of the enlisted soldier.

General officers rarely wore epaulets, dress hats, and waist sashes in the field during the Civil War, and many omitted even their swords and sword belts. Grant almost habitually left his coat unbuttoned to show a dark-blue vest, white shirt, and black cravat, and others followed suit. Although rare, elaborate non-regulation uniforms were worn by a few generals.

THE GENERAL STAFF AND STAFF CORPS

The General Staff and Staff Corps were responsible to general officers and for their various departments. The adjutants-general were chief assistants to general officers. One of the Army's oldest logistics branches, the Quartermaster Department was established by the Continental Congress on June 16, 1775, and supervised stores or barracks and distributed uniforms, supplies, and provisions to the troops. Responsible for construction projects such as forts, bridges, and roads, the Corps of Engineers was established on the same day.

Created as a civilian responsibility in July 1775, the position of Surgeon-General was given a military rank in 1836. Also established in 1775 was the position of Paymaster-General. The position of Commissary-General was originally created in 1777 with responsibility for feeding the troops. Charged with ensuring their combat readiness, the position of Inspector-General was created during the same year.

The Ordnance Department was established in 1812 to arm and equip the Army as a result of the War of 1812 (1812–15). At the peak of the Civil War, it numbered 64 officers, most of whom were assigned to divisions and above, while about 600 enlisted men, including ordnance sergeants, served at arsenals and depots. Ordnance responsibilities were also given to soldiers with previous training as blacksmiths or some other ordnance-related skill. These men remained with their units but were provided with related tools from the Ordnance Department. As a result, thousands of soldiers were detailed to perform Ordnance duties during the Civil War (Rubis 2022: website).

Authorized on July 4, 1838, the small Corps of Topographical Engineers consisted only of officers who were handpicked from the US Military Academy at West Point, New York. They were tasked with mapping and the design and construction of Federal civil works such as coastal fortifications, lighthouses, and navigational routes.

Serving on the special and personal staff of general officers, the position of Judge Advocate was created in 1775, but there were an insufficient number of officers assigned to legal duties to constitute a department until July 1862, following which the Bureau of Military Justice was established in June 1864. Originally established in 1776, the position of Provost Marshal General was required only in wartime and was revived on March 3, 1863, to deal with recruitment and desertion issues. It also supervised the Invalid Corps in which disabled soldiers performed garrison duty.

To all these were added aides-de-camp who were detailed from line regiments to serve on a general officer's personal staff.

Staff officers were prescribed the same pattern of dark-blue frock coat with skirts the same length as that for general and line officers in 1861, except for their collar and cuffs which were of the same material as the rest of the coat. Gilt buttons were of "General Staff" pattern, except for Corps of Engineers, Corps of Topographical Engineers, and Ordnance Department personnel, who wore the buttons of their respective corps. The buttons of the Corps of Engineers bore an eagle with an "ESSAYONS" (Let Us Try) scroll in its beak above a fort and rising sun. Those worn by the Corps of Topographical Engineers until at least 1863 bore a Union shield below which were the letters "TE" in

These details from Plate 172 of the *Atlas to Accompany the Official Records of the Union and Confederate Armies 1861–1865* show the large buttons worn by officers of the Corps of Engineers (above), Ordnance Department (middle), and the Corps of Topographical Engineers (below). (Author's collection)

Photographed while serving as Military Secretary to Major General Winfield Scott sometime between January 1, 1860, and April 12, 1861, Lieutenant Colonel Erasmus D. Keyes holds a *chapeau*, or cocked hat, which again became optional wear by generals and staff officers via General Orders No. 3. He wears the double-breasted frock coat with seven buttons in each row, which was regulation for field-grade officers from 1851 through 1872. On May 14, 1861, Keyes was given command of the 11th Infantry. (National Portrait Gallery, Smithsonian Institution; Frederick Hill Meserve Collection NPG.81.M1010)

Old English script. Those of the Ordnance Department bore a garter inscribed "ORDNANCE CORPS" superimposed over crossed cannon barrels.

Trousers were also dark blue with a ⅛in.-wide gold cord welt on the outer seam. For dress purposes headgear could consist of a *chapeau*, or Pattern 1858 hat the same as for general officers, being looped up on the right side with an embroidered Pattern 1858 "eagle" insignia on a black velvet ground, but with a cord of black silk and gold and acorn-shaped ends (*Regulations* 1861: 8). On the Pattern 1858 hat, all wore the same insignia as general officers, except for the aforementioned three corps and departments, which had their own distinctive devices. That of the Corps of Engineers consisted of an embroidered "turreted castle" in a wreath. The Corps of Topographical Engineers had an embroidered shield within a wreath, while the Ordnance Department wore an embroidered "flaming bomb" insignia. Forage caps were also worn with the same system of insignia at the front.

Epaulets for staff officers were the same pattern as for general officers, but attached to the strap were the silver letters "MS" ("Medical Staff") and "PD" in Old English script within a gold embroidered wreath for the Medical Department and Pay Department respectively. Corps of Engineers personnel wore a silver "turreted castle," Corps of Topographical Engineers personnel a gold embroidered shield with silver embroidered letters "TE," and Ordnance Department personnel a silver embroidered shell and flame.

Staff officers wore the same pattern of "cloak coat" as general officers with five braids of black silk arranged in a knot on each sleeve.

Staff officers wore black leather sword belts and crimson silk net waist sashes, except officers of the Medical Department, whose sashes were emerald green. The epaulets of the Medical, Pay, and Ordnance departments, the Corps of Engineers, and the Corps of Topographical Engineers had distinctive insignia as per 1851 Regulations. Medical Department and Pay Department staff had the letters "MS" and "PM" respectively embroidered in Old English script in a wreath. Ordnance Department staff had an embroidered "flaming bomb" within a wreath.

Corps of Engineers staff had a silver metal "turreted castle" insignia, while Corps of Topographical Engineers staff had a gold embroidered shield above the silver metallic letters "TE" in Old English script with a small star in between. Other staff officers, and aides-de-camp, had plain straps within the crescent.

When not in full dress, staff officers wore gold-bordered shoulder straps with a dark-blue ground, with the rank of colonel indicated by a silver embroidered eagle at its center, lieutenant colonel by a silver embroidered leaf at each end, major by a gold embroidered leaf at each end, captain by two gold embroidered bars at each end, first lieutenant by one gold embroidered bar at each end, and second lieutenant by a plain strap. By 1864, the rank of some staff officers appears to have been shown by insignia embroidered directly on the shoulders of the coat rather than in a strap.

Most staff officers carried either the Model 1850 sword with slightly curved blade, or the purely decorative Model 1860 sword with straight blade. The exceptions were swords of the Quartermaster Department, and the Medical and Pay departments, which had "MS" and "PD" respectively on decorative quillons.

In reality, the clothing of staff officers often varied considerably from regulation and was dependent on what their commanding general might require. Some expected uniformity while others cared little what their staff and assistants wore, permitting sack coats, blouses, and jackets of all styles.

General Orders No. 286 permitted officers of all departments serving in the field to dispense with shoulder straps and wear the mark of rank sewn directly on to their shoulders or coat lapels. The same order allowed them to wear overcoats of the same color and pattern as those of enlisted men. They could also dispense with ornaments on overcoats, hats, or forage caps, and not wear epaulets and sashes (*General Orders ... Volunteer Force* 1865: 170). To some extent this order may have been issued to reduce the conspicuousness of the officers when under fire.

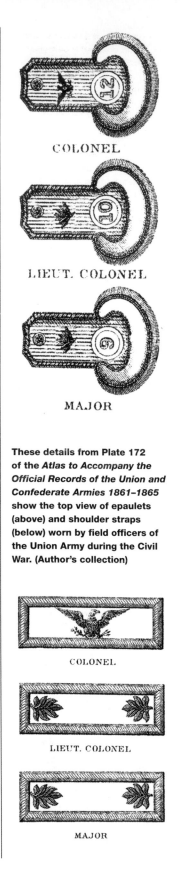

COLONEL

LIEUT. COLONEL

MAJOR

These details from Plate 172 of the *Atlas to Accompany the Official Records of the Union and Confederate Armies 1861–1865* show the top view of epaulets (above) and shoulder straps (below) worn by field officers of the Union Army during the Civil War. (Author's collection)

COLONEL.

LIEUT. COLONEL.

MAJOR.

INFANTRY

In April 1861, the infantry of the US Army consisted of ten regiments composed of ten companies each, the rolls of which included about 8,000 officers and men. The outbreak of the Civil War reduced the effectiveness of these units almost immediately, as approximately one-third of the officer corps resigned to join the Confederacy. Few NCOs and enlisted men joined them, however, as many were foreign-born and had little attachment to the Confederate states.

Stationed in Texas when the conflict began, the 1st Infantry fought in the Mississippi area of operations, one of its first battles being at Wilson's Creek, Missouri, on August 10, 1861. It campaigned with Grant against Vicksburg, Mississippi, in May–July 1863, and ended the war occupying New Orleans, Louisiana. Transferred to the Midwest in 1861, elements of the 2d Infantry fought at the First Battle of Bull Run, Virginia, on July 21, 1861, and also at Wilson's Creek. After being assigned to the Army of the Potomac, the regiment formed part of the infantry brigade commanded by Brigadier General George Sykes, known as "Sykes' Regulars," and went on to fight throughout all the major Eastern campaigns of the Civil War.

Most of the 3d Infantry was serving in Florida when the Civil War began, while the 7th and 10th Infantry were in New Mexico, and the 4th and 6th Infantry were on the West Coast. All of these regiments transferred east, where elements of them served in "Sykes' Regulars."

The 5th Infantry remained throughout the war in New Mexico. Four companies of the regiment formed the rearguard during the Union retreat leading to the battle of Valverde on February 21, 1862, while two of its companies captured a field piece at Glorieta Pass on March 28, 1862. After capture in Texas, and reorganization in May 1861, the 8th Infantry served as provost guard in the Union camps at Gettysburg, and performed similar duties until 1865. The 9th Infantry remained in California on provost guard duty throughout the Civil War.

On May 14, 1861, President Lincoln acted to augment the ranks of the US infantry via General Orders No. 33, which directed an increase in the size of the Regular Army to include nine new infantry regiments officially consisting of three battalions of eight companies each, amounting to 20,000 soldiers. The battalions within these regiments often operated independently of each other. The 11th, 12th, 14th, and 17th Infantry joined "Sykes' Regulars" and participated in most of the major campaigns in the East. The other five regiments saw extensive action in the Midwest.

The infantry officer's Pattern 1858 hat was looped up on the right side with an embroidered Pattern 1858 "eagle" insignia on a black velvet ground; other trimmings were the same as for General Staff except for the ornament at the front, which consisted of "a gold embroidered bugle, on black velvet ground, with the number of the regiment in silver within the bend" (*Regulations* 1861: 8). This was fitted on an oval-shaped tin plate with wire loops on the back for easy removal from the hat. Officers below the rank of field officer wore only two black ostrich feathers. As a result of General Orders No. 3, field officers serving as staff officers could also wear a *chapeau*, or cocked hat.

Field-grade infantry officers were prescribed for full dress a Pattern 1851 frock coat of the same length as for General Staff personnel, with two rows of seven "eagle I" buttons for colonel, lieutenant colonel,

This example of a Pattern 1858 hat for an enlisted infantryman conforms to General Orders No. 4, which required the brim to be looped up on the left side only for infantry enlisted men. Ornamentation consists of a Pattern 1858 brass "eagle" plate looping up the brim; a die-struck "looped infantry horn" and company letter at the front; a single black ostrich feather on the right of the crown; and sky-blue worsted cord. Regimental numbers required to be fastened within the loop of the horn insignia are missing. (Smithsonian Institution NMAH AF.25124.021)

and major, and a single row of nine buttons of the same type for captains, plus first and second lieutenants.

Full-dress epaulets for a colonel of infantry had a gold bullion strap and fringe of the same width and length as for General Staff personnel, but with the regimental number embroidered in gold within a circlet of embroidered silver with a sky-blue ground inside the crescent, and a silver embroidered "spread eagle" at the center of the strap. A lieutenant colonel and major of infantry both wore the same pattern of epaulet as a colonel, but substituting the eagle for a silver embroidered leaf on the strap.

Epaulets for an infantry captain were the same, but with bullion ¼in. in diameter and 2½in. long, while the strap had two silver embroidered bars. Epaulets for first lieutenant were the same, but with bullion ⅛in. in diameter and one silver embroidered bar. Those for second lieutenant were the same but with a plain strap. When not in full dress, infantry officers wore gold-bordered shoulder straps bearing the same configuration of embroidered insignia as for staff officers, but on a light- or sky-blue ground.

Trousers for infantry regimental officers were dark blue with a ⅛in.-wide sky-blue welt in the outside seam.

For dress occasions, infantry colonels wore the same pattern of "cloak coat" as general officers with five braids of black silk arranged in a single knot on each sleeve. Lieutenant colonels wore four braids; majors, three braids; captains, two braids; first lieutenants, one braid; and second lieutenants and brevet second lieutenants, plain sleeves without braid or knot. The same applied to officers in all other branches of service.

Privately purchased, the sword-belt plate for infantry officers was Pattern 1851 with a rectangular raised rim containing a silver wreath of laurel encircling the coat of arms of the United States consisting of an eagle, shield, scroll, edge of cloud, stars, and sun rays. The scroll bore the motto "E PLURIBUS UNUM" (Out of Many, One). Infantry NCOs also had Pattern 1851 plates on belts supporting their swords. Worn with a crimson silk net waist sash for dress occasions, the sword belt for infantry officers and NCOs was of plain black leather.

This detail from Plate 172 of the *Atlas to Accompany the Official Records of the Union and Confederate Armies 1861–1865* shows the "eagle I" button worn by Union Army infantry officers. (Author's collection)

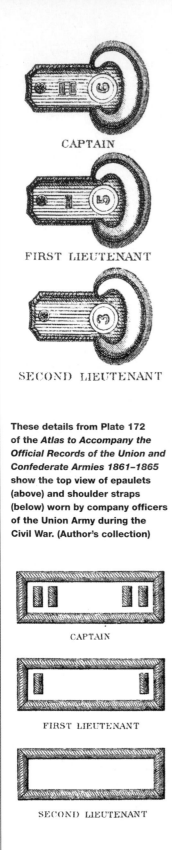

CAPTAIN

FIRST LIEUTENANT

SECOND LIEUTENANT

These details from Plate 172 of the *Atlas to Accompany the Official Records of the Union and Confederate Armies 1861–1865* show the top view of epaulets (above) and shoulder straps (below) worn by company officers of the Union Army during the Civil War. (Author's collection)

CAPTAIN

FIRST LIEUTENANT

SECOND LIEUTENANT

For field dress, some infantry officers wore privately purchased and tailored four-button sack coats with shoulder straps displaying rank. This type of garment often had narrow black twill trim on the front and lower hem and around the collar, and was partially lined with polished cotton. Others infantry officers occasionally had a frock coat converted to a jacket by removing the skirts.

The black felt dress hat worn by infantry enlisted men was inferior in quality to that of officers, and was the only such headgear with the brim looped up on the left side (as per General Orders No. 4) with a Pattern 1858 brass "eagle" plate. The brim had a double row of stitching rather than being edged with silk binding. Trimmings consisted of a Pattern 1858 brass, 3½in.-wide "looped infantry horn" attached to the front of the crown via two narrow prongs, with ⅝in.-tall brass regimental numbers within the loop, and a 1in.-tall company letter above; a single black ostrich feather on the right of the crown; and a sky-blue worsted cord terminating in two 2in.-long tassels on the side opposite the feather.

The uniform coat worn by all infantry NCOs and enlisted men was a dark-blue single-breasted frock coat with skirt extending to "one-half the distance from the top of the hip to the bend of the knee" (*Regulations* 1861: 8). Nine large-size buttons at the front, and two small ones at each cuff plus the tops of pockets in the folds of the skirt, were of "General Service" pattern without stars or border. The standing collar and pointed cuffs were trimmed with a sky-blue welt or cord. Some infantrymen were photographed wearing coats with lowered collars and trim along the bottom edge only.

For dress occasions, infantry enlisted men wore metallic shoulder scales. First introduced in 1851 for Dragoons and Light Artillery, presumably to protect the shoulders during a saber fight, these were issued to men of all branches of service by 1854. That for privates consisted of seven scalloped surfaces on a 2⅕in.-wide edged strap with a rounded end and a half-round, 4in.-wide crescent. A sergeant's scale had a strap of the same dimensions, but its crescent was 4½in. wide and fully rounded in profile. A third pattern similar to that of NCOs was worn by noncommissioned staff; this had three small, rounded rivets on each of six of its scallops, making 18 rivets in total. Scales were secured to the coat by means of long, open brass straps that passed through cloth or brass loops attached to the shoulder of the coat and slotted over brass staples sewn on near the collar. Also for dress occasions, most infantry musicians wore a "herringbone" pattern of ⅜in.-wide sky-blue lace on the front of the coat.

Trousers were fly-fronted and of dark-blue cloth. Those worn by sergeants were distinguished by a 1½in.-wide sky-blue worsted welt on the outer seams, and corporals by a ½in.-wide welt. Via General Orders No. 108, issued on December 16, 1861, sky-blue trousers with dark-blue seam stripes of the same dimensions were ordered to be worn, and began to replace those of dark blue for all branches of service, although some regular troops may have worn dark-blue trousers for as long as they were serviceable.

Originally prescribed for fatigue use by mounted troops, the four-button sack coat was approved for fatigue duties for the infantry, and all other branches of service, via General Orders No. 3. With the urgent

need for uniforms in 1861, the sack coat could be made more quickly and cheaply than the frock coat and became an important part of the uniform of both regular and volunteer troops in the Union Army. Described as being "of dark blue flannel extending half way down the thigh, and made loose, without sleeve or body lining" (*Regulations* 1861: 5), it had a falling collar and an inside pocket on the left side. Although those prescribed for recruits were intended to have sleeve and body lining, all troops were sometimes issued lined sack coats during cold weather.

Also originally prescribed for fatigue purposes, but worn regularly in lieu of the dress hat, forage caps were authorized on November 29, 1858. On April 11, 1859, Pattern 1851 cloth dress caps were authorized to be converted into forage caps by the removal of stiffening in the crown. Forage caps were generally described as being of "Dark blue cloth, with a welt of the same around the crown, and yellow metal letters in front to designate companies" (*Regulations* 1861: 8–9). Extant examples also bear regimental numbers, however. The crown of the Pattern 1858 cap was flat and stiffened inside with cardboard, and stood about 4½in. above the line of the visor. The earliest examples produced at the Schuylkill Arsenal in Philadelphia, Pennsylvania, had a stiff horizontal leather visor, but with mass production by outside contractors during 1861–65 this was replaced by a curved visor of glazed leather, which tended to point up or down when worn (Gaede 1999: 68).

Of sky-blue kersey, the overcoat for foot troops was single-breasted with seven small-size "General Service" buttons, a standing collar that could also be worn turned down, and a cape that reached to the elbow. Although regulations required the placement of NCOs' chevrons above the elbow on the sleeves of overcoats, this practice is seldom visible in photographs of the period due to the presence of the cape.

Footwear for infantry enlisted men consisted of "Jefferson" boots, or brogans, of left and right pattern.

ARTILLERY

Four artillery regiments, each of 12 batteries, existed before the Civil War. Until 1861, only two batteries within each regiment served as light artillery; the others were on detached coastal or garrison service. Batteries E and H of the 1st Artillery garrisoned Fort Sumter in Charleston Harbor, South Carolina, under Major Robert Anderson during the bombardment on April 12–13, 1861. Following reorganization for war, the whole of the 1st and 4th Artillery were converted to light artillery, while all but three batteries of the 2d Artillery and two of the 3d Artillery served as light artillery. Battery M of the 2d Artillery, commanded by Second Lieutenant Peter C. Hains, fired the first shot by the Union Army at First Bull Run. Initially concentrated on the West Coast at San Francisco, batteries of the 3d Artillery later saw separate action in the Midwest and East Theater. Battery B of the 4th Artillery formed part of the vaunted Iron Brigade in the Army of the Potomac.

On May 14, 1861, a new regiment of 12 batteries was added to this branch of service. The 5th Artillery was constituted on June 18, 1861, and organized at Camp Greble, Pennsylvania. Differing in composition from the older regiments, it was composed of light artillery only, and was the first entire Regular Army regiment so clothed and equipped.

The artillery officer's dress hat was looped up on the right side with an embroidered Pattern 1858 "eagle" insignia on a black velvet ground, and had at the front a gold embroidered "crossed cannon" insignia on a black velvet ground, with the regimental number in silver at the intersection of the cannon.

As with the infantry, regimental-grade artillery officers wore for dress uniform the Pattern 1851 frock coat, in their case with two rows of seven "eagle A" buttons for colonel, lieutenant colonel, and major, and a single row of nine for captains, first lieutenants, and second lieutenants.

Epaulets for an artillery colonel had a gold bullion fringe of the same width and length as for infantry officers, but with a scarlet strap and

These details from Plate 172 of the *Atlas to Accompany the Official Records of the Union and Confederate Armies 1861–1865* show the large "eagle A" button worn by Union artillery officers (above) and (below) the chevrons worn by sergeant majors of the Regulars and Volunteers. (Author's collection)

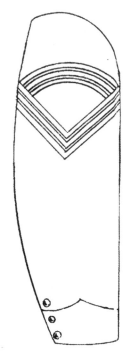

Dressed in scarlet-trimmed Pattern 1854 mounted service jackets with shoulder scales attached, and "crossed cannon" insignia on their cap tops, these regular artillerists were photographed at the Light Artillery Depot of the XX Corps at Washington, DC, in 1865. (Library of Congress LC-DIG-ppmsca-34095)

gold embroidered regimental number within a circlet of embroidered silver inside the crescent, plus a silver embroidered "spread eagle" at the center of the strap. A lieutenant colonel and major of artillery wore the same pattern of epaulet, but with a silver embroidered leaf on the scarlet strap. Epaulets for an artillery captain were the same as for higher-grade officers, but with bullion ¼in. in diameter and 2½in. long; the scarlet strap had two silver embroidered bars. Epaulets for an artillery first lieutenant had bullion ⅛in. in diameter and one silver embroidered bar, while those for second lieutenant had a plain scarlet strap. Gold-bordered scarlet shoulder straps were worn by all artillery officers with the same embroidered insignia commensurate with rank.

A jacket for light-artillery officers was introduced via General Orders No. 20 on August 6, 1860. This was described as a dark-blue jacket, "trimmed with scarlet, with the Russian shoulder-knot, the prescribed insignia of rank … worked in silver in the center of the knot" (*Regulations* 1861: 4). Trousers were dark blue with a ⅛in.-wide scarlet welt in the outside seam. Pattern 1851 rectangular "eagle" plates fastened the plain black leather sword belts for artillery officers and NCOs.

Looped up on the right side with a brass "eagle" plate, the dress hat for enlisted men serving as heavy artillery had a Pattern 1858 brass "crossed cannon" insignia at the front of the crown, with a 1in. company letter and ⅝in. regimental number above, plus scarlet worsted cord around the crown ending with two tassels on the opposite side from a single black ostrich feather.

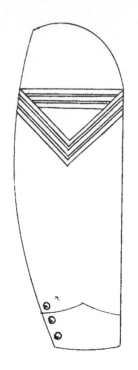

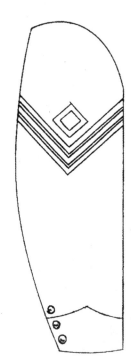

These details from Plate 172 of the *Atlas to Accompany the Official Records of the Union and Confederate Armies 1861–1865* show the sleeve insignia worn by quartermaster sergeants (above) and first sergeants (below) of the Regulars and Volunteers. (Author's collection)

A dress cap had been authorized for light-artillery companies, which was patterned on the Ringgold Light Artillery Shako designed *c.*1837 by Major Samuel B. Ringgold, who was killed during the Mexican–American War (1846–48). Described as consisting of the "old pattern uniform cap, with red horse-hair plume, cord and tassel" (*Regulations* 1861: 8), this headgear seldom seems to have been worn, and with the outbreak of the Civil War could hardly have been more unsuitable for field or combat wear, with light-artillery units preferring the Pattern 1858 hat or forage cap.

Often posted in garrison as heavy artillery, enlisted men wore dress uniforms complete with shoulder scales more regularly than other branches of service. On these occasions, the uniform coat worn by all NCOs and enlisted men of the 1st through 4th Artillery was the same pattern as for infantry, but with scarlet trim around the collar and cuffs. Likewise, artillery musicians wore a "herringbone" pattern of scarlet lace on the front of the coat.

When serving as light artillery, companies of the 1st through 4th Artillery wore for dress the Pattern 1854 mounted service jacket with a single row of 12 small "General Service" buttons at the front and two on each cuff; a standing collar edged with scarlet wool trim and with two scarlet false buttonholes either side; and scarlet-trimmed back-seams, cuffs, edging, and rear bolsters.

Until December 16, 1861, the trousers of enlisted men serving as heavy artillery were officially prescribed as dark-blue cloth, with those for sergeants having 1½in.-wide scarlet seam stripes, and ½in. wide for corporals. Sky-blue trousers with scarlet seam stripes for NCOs and a reinforced seat and inner leg for all were authorized for issue to light artillery enlisted men on August 6, 1860.

In the field and on campaign, plain dark-blue four-button sack coats were often worn by enlisted men of these regiments. Forage caps were mostly Pattern 1858, and the sky-blue double-breasted mounted man's overcoat with cape that reached to the cuffs of the sleeves was worn by the men of light-artillery companies.

Field- and company-grade officers of the 5th Artillery wore the same dress uniform as the other four regiments. The enlisted men of the 5th Artillery wore for dress the uniform jacket, Pattern 1858 dress hat, and sky-blue trousers with scarlet seam stripes according to rank; and for campaign duty sack coats and forage caps.

Issuance of a new-pattern light-artillery dress cap occurred in 1864, possibly due to some light-artillery batteries being assigned to garrison duty or serving as occupation forces. The cap was produced as a result of a contract let out on January 29, 1864, for 1,452 light-artillery uniform caps for the use of both regulars and volunteer troops (Howell 1975: 23).

Also available at this time was an officer-pattern plumed dress cap with a body of dark-blue pressed felt with beaver-fur finish, and with leather trim on the crown, around the base, and visor. The insignia at the front consisted of gold embroidered crossed cannon with the regimental number in silver at the intersection of the cannon. Above this was a gold and silver embroidered hat "eagle." The red horsehair plume had a woven wool worsted base supported by a short brass "flaming bomb" tulip. A bullion cord was draped fore and aft, and a bullion plaque and tassel was attached to the coat or jacket.

DRAGOONS, MOUNTED RIFLEMEN, AND CAVALRY

The regular mounted regiments entered the Civil War as the 1st and 2d Dragoons, Regiment of Mounted Riflemen, and 1st and 2d Cavalry regiments. The 3d Cavalry was organized at Pittsburgh, Pennsylvania, on May 3, 1861. Since 1854 it had been advocated to redesignate all of these regiments as cavalry, and to renumber them in order of seniority. On August 3, 1861, this was finally done via Act of Congress. As a result, the 1st and 2d Dragoons became the 1st and 2d Cavalry, the Regiment of Mounted Riflemen became the 3d Cavalry, and the 1st, 2nd, and recently organized 3d Cavalry became the 4th, 5th, and 6th Cavalry respectively.

The dragoon officer's dress hat was looped up on the right side with an embroidered Pattern 1858 "eagle" insignia on a black velvet ground, while the insignia at the front consisted of gold embroidered "crossed sabers," edges up, on a black velvet ground with the regimental number in silver in the upper angle.

Since 1856, officers of the 1st and 2d Dragoons wore for full dress the Pattern 1851 frock coat with two rows of seven "eagle D" buttons for colonel, lieutenant colonel, and major, and a single row of nine buttons of the same type for captains, first lieutenants, and second lieutenants. Full-dress epaulets for a colonel of dragoons had a gold bullion fringe of the same width and length as for general officers, but with an orange strap and the regimental number embroidered in gold within a circlet of embroidered silver inside the crescent, and a silver embroidered "spread eagle" at the center of the strap. A lieutenant colonel and major of dragoons wore the same pattern of epaulet as a colonel, but substituting the "spread eagle" for a silver embroidered leaf on the strap.

Epaulets for a dragoon captain were the same but with bullion ¼in. in diameter and 2⅛in. long, while the strap had two silver embroidered bars. Epaulets for first lieutenant were the same but with bullion ⅛in. in diameter and 2½in. long and one silver embroidered bar; those for second lieutenant were the same but with a plain strap. For undress duties, gold-bordered shoulder straps were worn by all dragoon officers and bore the same configuration of embroidered insignia on an orange field.

Trousers for dragoon regimental officers were dark blue with a ⅛in.-wide orange welt in the outside seam. All dragoon officers and NCOs

This detail from Plate 172 of the *Atlas to Accompany the Official Records of the Union and Confederate Armies 1861–1865* shows the "eagle C" button worn by Union Army cavalry officers. The buttons of officers of mounted riflemen and dragoons were of similar pattern, but with "R" or "D" respectively in the shield. (Author's collection)

Photographed at Brandy Station, Virginia, in February 1864, the enlisted men of this detachment of the 1st Cavalry wear a mixture of mounted service jackets and sack coats. The officer at right of center wears a cutdown frock coat with the skirts removed. The officer in the light-colored overcoat, top-boots, and gauntlets is Second Lieutenant Camillo C.C. Carr. (US Army Heritage & Education Center MOLLUS 35_1720)

wore a black leather sword belt fastened by a Pattern 1851 rectangular "eagle" plate, underneath which was worn a crimson silk net waist sash for dress occasions.

The dress hat for enlisted dragoons was of the same pattern as that for officers, but looped up on the right side with a stamped-metal "eagle" plate, and with Pattern 1858 brass "crossed sabers" insignia, scabbard tips up, at the front, plus the company letter above and regimental number below; the hat also bore one black ostrich feather attached to the left side of the crown, and an orange worsted cord with two tassels.

For full dress, enlisted men of the dragoon regiments were prescribed dark-blue Pattern 1854 uniform jackets bound with orange lace around the collar, cuffs, and back seams, and fastened by 12 small "General Service" buttons at the front and two on each cuff. The standing collar also had two orange false buttonholes terminating in buttons of the same pattern on each side. Brass shoulder scales were worn with this jacket.

Since 1858, trousers were dark blue with orange worsted lace seam stripes for NCOs, 1½in. wide for sergeants and ½in. wide for corporals. These were later replaced by sky-blue trousers with the same color and width of seam stripes. For both officers and enlisted men of the dragoon regiments, the trousers had a reinforced seat and inner leg. Fatigue wear for enlisted dragoons consisted of dark-blue Pattern 1858 four-button sack coats and plain dark-blue forage caps.

Both dragoon regiments were armed with Sharps carbines, Colt Army and Navy revolvers, and a mixture of Model 1840 and Model 1860 sabers.

Raised specially to guard the Oregon Trail, the Regiment of Mounted Riflemen by 1861 wore much the same pattern of uniform as dragoons with the exception of dress-hat insignia, buttons, and branch-of-service-colored emerald-green trim on officers' epaulet straps and shoulder

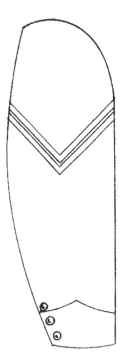

These details from Plate 172 of the *Atlas to Accompany the Official Records of the Union and Confederate Armies 1861–1865* show the sleeve insignia worn by sergeants (above) and corporals (below) of the Union Army. (Author's collection)

straps. The device on the front of the officers' hat was a perpendicular, gold embroidered trumpet on a black velvet ground. This was also sometimes worn at the front of officers' undress caps. That for enlisted men was a die-stamped insignia of the same pattern. Buttons on officers' frock coats were of the large "eagle R" pattern, while enlisted men wore "General Service" buttons. Officers' dark-blue trousers had a ⅛in.-wide green welt in the outer seams. Those of NCOs were the same as for dragoons but with a green welt. As with the dragoons, trousers for both officers and enlisted men had a reinforced seat and inner leg. Pattern 1854 jackets worn by enlisted men were trimmed with green while trousers were plain dark blue, later sky blue.

At the outbreak of the Civil War the mounted riflemen were armed with a mixture of Model 1841 rifles and First Model Maynard carbines (McAulay 1996: 11). These were exchanged for Sharps carbines in early 1862 (McAulay 2003: 91).

When all the mounted regiments of the regular army were consolidated into one corps in August 1861, the dragoons and mounted riflemen were officially required to wear the yellow-trimmed uniforms prescribed for US cavalry. Of that occasion, however, First Lieutenant Theophilus F. Rodenbaugh, Co. A, 2d Dragoons, wrote:

> Alas! For the cherished "orange," it must give place to the gaudy yellow; "but the troops," so read the order, "will be permitted to wear out the clothing now on hand." The marvellous durability of orange facings, or the prodigious quantity of similar clothing "on hand" in the "Second," enabled that regiment to postpone for more than two years the thorough execution of the order; and, when eventually forced to "change their stripes," the depressing effect might have readily caused an ignorant civilian to look upon yellow cloth as military mourning. (Rodenbaugh 1875: 237–38)

Doubtless the 1st Dragoons and Mounted Riflemen also had permission to wear out their old uniforms before adopting cavalry yellow.

The uniform worn by the 1st and 2d Cavalry, and newly organized 3d Cavalry, which became the 4th, 5th, and 6th Cavalry respectively in August 1861 was mostly the same as that worn by the two dragoon regiments and the Regiment of Mounted Riflemen. Like the 1st and 2d Dragoons, dress hats worn by cavalry officers were looped up on the right side with an embroidered Pattern 1858 "eagle" insignia on a black velvet ground, and were distinguished by two gold embroidered "crossed sabers," scabbard tips up, on a black velvet ground, but with the regimental number below in silver. Hat cords were gold with gold acorn-shaped ends. Epaulets on frock coats had a yellow strap, and shoulder straps for less formal wear had a yellow ground. Buttons on frock coats were of "eagle C" pattern, while dark-blue trousers had a ⅛in.-wide yellow welt in the outer seams and a reinforced seat.

Cavalry officers and those serving with mounted troops often wore in the field dark-blue jackets prescribed for stable duty. The jackets worn by enlisted cavalrymen were of the same pattern as for dragoons, mounted riflemen, and light artillery, but trimmed with yellow lace. Dark-blue trousers were replaced by those of sky blue with a reinforced seat and inner leg after December 1861, and sergeants and corporals were distinguished by 1½in.- and ½in.-wide seam stripes respectively. The dress hat for enlisted cavalry was of the same pattern as that for enlisted dragoons, being looped up on the right side, and with Pattern 1858 brass "crossed sabers," edges up, and yellow worsted cord and tassels. Fatigue wear was also the same as for enlisted dragoons.

All enlisted cavalrymen wore the sky-blue double-breasted mounted man's overcoat with a cape that reached to the cuffs of the sleeves.

UNITED STATES COLORED TROOPS

African Americans, and troops recruited from other minority groups, constituted about 10 percent of the manpower of the Union Army. About 20 percent of these personnel died of disease, wounds, or in battle; many fought with distinction, with 16 awarded the Medal of Honor, although none received formal recognition and medals until the beginning of the 20th century.

Organized as a result of the Confiscation Act of 1862, which freed enslaved persons whose owners were in rebellion against the United States, and the Militia Act of 1862, which empowered the President to use former enslaved persons in any capacity in the Union Army, units such as the 1st South Carolina Volunteer Infantry, US Colored Troops, and the Corps d'Afrique were composed primarily of African American soldiers, although they also included men from other minority groups. Formed in mid-1863, the Corps d'Afrique contained at its maximum strength 25 infantry regiments, five engineer regiments, one cavalry regiment, and one heavy-artillery regiment.

In April 1864 these units were incorporated into a single corps designated the United States Colored Troops (USCT), which contained 135 infantry regiments composed of the 1st–138th USCT, although the 94th, 105th, and 126th USCT were never fully formed, plus one

Worn by Private John Clark, Co. A, 8th USC Heavy Artillery, this mounted service jacket was made at the Schuylkill Arsenal in Philadelphia, Pennsylvania, and issued to him following his enlistment on September 30, 1864. The issuance and wearing of jackets by both black and white heavy artillerymen was quite common, possibly due to lower production costs involved in making a jacket as opposed to a frock coat, or the greater comfort of the wearer by not having coat tails. This jacket has the regulation number of small "General Service" buttons on the front, collar, and cuffs. Toward the middle of the bottom edge of its back can be seen the cloth bolsters designed to support the weight of an artillery saber belt that carried the pistol and saber of a mounted soldier. Clark's name and unit are stenciled on the lining at the neck. As a result of his civilian occupation, Clark served as the regimental blacksmith. He died of scurvy on July 23, 1865. (Dr. Michael R. Cunningham collection)

ABOVE LEFT
This unidentified cavalry sergeant of the USCT wears a Pattern 1861 forage cap, Pattern 1854 mounted service jacket partially colorized with yellow trim, and mounted service trousers with a reinforced seat and inner leg. His belt is fastened with a Pattern 1851 rectangular gilt "eagle" plate, and he holds a Model 1860 light-cavalry saber. (Library of Congress LC-DIG-ppmsca-37027)

ABOVE RIGHT
This unidentified private of Co. B, 103d USCT, wears a frock coat with sky-blue infantry trim and brass shoulder scales. His forage cap top has brass insignia indicating his unit, which has been painted over by the photographer or his colorist. (Library of Congress LC-DIG-ppmsca-36988)

independent regiment of infantry known as Powell's Regiment, USCT; one unassigned company of infantry designated Co. A, USCT; and one independent company of infantry. There were also six mounted regiments designated 1st–6th USC Cavalry; 13 heavy-artillery regiments composed of the 1st and 3rd–14th USC Heavy Artillery; the 2d USC Light Artillery; and one independent heavy-artillery battery.

Excluded from the USCT were six African American units designated as regulars. Formed in Massachusetts and Connecticut, their men were credited to these states' quota, no matter where they were recruited. These included the 5th Regiment Massachusetts Colored Volunteer Cavalry; the 54th and 55th Massachusetts (Colored) Volunteer Infantry regiments; and the 29th, 30th, and 31st Connecticut (Colored) Volunteer Infantry regiments.

Field- and company-grade white officers appointed to Corps d'Afrique and USCT regiments wore regulation uniforms. Although enlisted men of several of the earlier African American regiments were provided with distinctive clothing, from 1863 all were issued with US regulation branch-of-service dress uniforms plus fatigue clothing. As a rule, African American troops took readily to dress uniforms and followed the regulations more closely to include brass shoulder scales. While Pattern 1858 black felt dress hats were issued to the Corps d'Afrique, they were seldom worn by USCT personnel. Some regiments recruited in the Midwest wore short nine-button jackets for full dress. The only indication of special uniforms is found in a letter from the Army Clothing & Equipage Office to the Quartermaster General dated March 3, 1864, which reported the issue of undersize "French zouave clothing" to the "Musicians and Bands of Colored Regiments" (Todd 1977: 414).

UNITED STATES SHARPSHOOTERS

Originally envisioned as "a mounted rifle corps," the United States Sharpshooters (USSS) was organized in 1861 by Colonel Hiram Berdan, with "crack rifle shots" from all Northern states being recruited. As the response was greater than expected, two regiments were formed, plus two companies of Andrews Sharpshooters.

A report in July 1861 suggested the USSS uniform would be a "heavy, dark blue flannel sack coat, metal buttons, with black velvet collar, and brown hat with small black feather" (*PS*, July 11, 1861: 1:3). During the following month a more reliable report stated that their uniform would be "of gray cloth in winter and green in summer, these colors being similar to those of nature, and rendering the outlines of a man completely indistinguishable at a moderate distance" (*DFP*, August 9, 1861: 1:1). In his regimental history, Charles A. Stevens, formerly of Co. G, 1st USSS, wrote: "Our uniform was of fine material, consisting of dark green coat and cap with black plume, light blue trowsers (afterward exchanged for green ones) and leather leggins, presenting a striking contrast to the regular blue of the infantry …" (Stevens 1892: 5).

Headgear initially consisted of a patent waterproof "Havelock" hat. Made of a gray felt with a leather visor, it had a rear flap to cover the neck, and holes for ventilation. This headgear was discarded and replaced by a Pattern 1861 forage cap of dark-green cloth.

Worn over the green coats, winter clothing consisted of an "Austrian-gray overcoat" edged with green. According to Stevens, these were "likewise abandoned, although they were good rain shedders, only

Officer's cap insignia of the United States Sharpshooters. (Courtesy of the Company of Military Historians)

FAR LEFT
It is unclear whether officers of the United States Sharpshooters wore dark-green or regulation dark-blue uniforms, although Lieutenant Colonel William Y.W. Ripley wrote after the Civil War that green uniforms were worn by "officers and men alike" (Ripley 1803: 20). Photographed at the New York studio of Matthew B. Brady in 1862, Colonel Hiram Berdan holds a cap bearing an insignia consisting of a wreath inside which is a pair of crossed rifles with "US" above and "SS" below in Old English script on a black velvet oval backing cloth. Other officers of this corps likely wore the same insignia. The light color of Berdan's waist sash indicates it was probably buff or yellow and not scarlet. (US National Archives NARA – 111-B-2374)

LEFT
Private Sherrod Brown, Co. F, 1st USSS, wears a dark-green frock coat with black hard rubber "General Service" buttons. Worn over his lighter-colored trousers, which may have been sky blue, are leather leggings. He holds a Sharps New Model 1859 breech-loading rifle fitted with a triangular bayonet. (Library of Congress LC-DIG-ppmsca-75447)

they became when wet stiff as a board" (Stevens 1892: 40). By September 1863 all the gray overcoats had been replaced. According to Stevens, while the Sharpshooters were encamped near Culpeper, Virginia, during that period "a large amount of green clothing, with over-coats (which were the regulation blue) … were received and distributed" (Stevens 1892: 354). The plume and leggings soon followed, with neither surviving in any great quantity beyond 1862.

The original recruits were instructed to bring their own target rifles, but the first skirmishes with the enemy demonstrated that these weapons were unsuitable for combat. Instead, Berdan settled on the .52-caliber Sharps New Model 1859 breech-loading rifle as the best possible weapon. His requisition for this weapon initially met with resistance, however, until President Lincoln intervened in order that the United States Sharpshooters got the firearm Berdan desired. In the interim, Colt five-shot revolving rifles were issued in the Sharps' place. Supply of the Sharps rifles did not begin until April 1862, and was not complete for both regiments until May 24, 1862.

Regarding equipage, both regiments of Sharpshooters were issued standard accouterments, although brass plates were removed because of their reflective value. There were two exceptions: the cartridge box for the Sharps rifle, worn on the waist belt, which held two wooden blocks containing ten 1½in.-deep bored holes to contain separately the .52-caliber linen-encased ball fired by the Sharps rifle; and the leather knapsack, reminiscent of the pattern used by the Prussian Army.

INFANTRY
1: Infantry colonel, 1861
1a: "Infantry I" button
1b: Pattern 1851 officer's belt plate
2: Company musician, 2d Infantry, 1862
3: Corporal, 14th Infantry, 1864

A

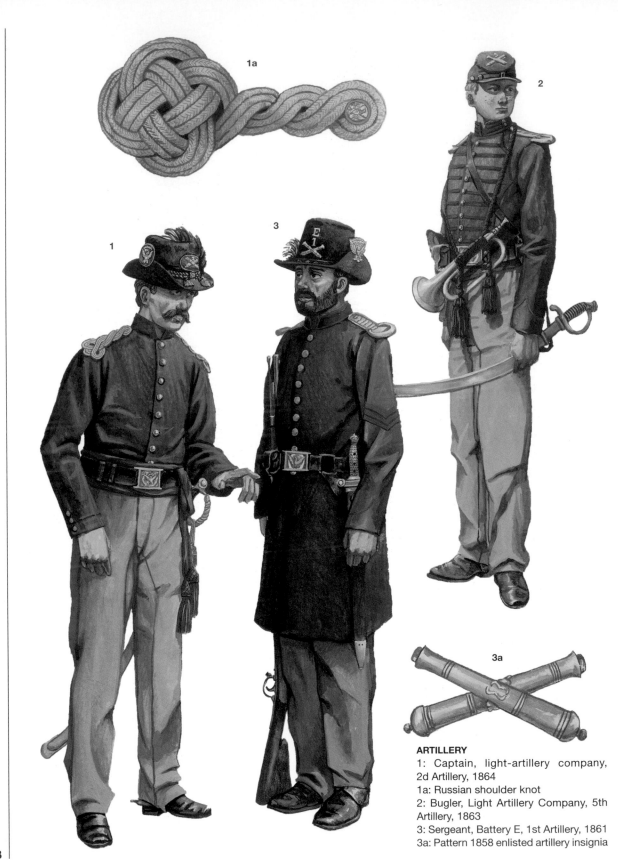

ARTILLERY

1: Captain, light-artillery company, 2d Artillery, 1864

1a: Russian shoulder knot

2: Bugler, Light Artillery Company, 5th Artillery, 1863

3: Sergeant, Battery E, 1st Artillery, 1861

3a: Pattern 1858 enlisted artillery insignia

B

DRAGOONS, MOUNTED RIFLEMEN, AND CAVALRY

1: Private, 2d Dragoons, 1862
2: Private, Regiment of Mounted Riflemen, 1861
3: First Lieutenant, 2d Cavalry, 1864
3a: "General Staff" button

1

2

3

3a

C

US COLORED TROOPS AND US SHARPSHOOTERS
1: Private, 12th Infantry, USCT, 1864
1a: Infantry horn insignia
1b: Pattern 1826 "eagle" plate
2: Private, 1st USSS, 1862
2a: "General Service"-pattern rubber button
3: Sergeant, 2d USSS, 1863

D

INVALID/VETERAN RESERVE CORPS AND US INDIAN HOME GUARD
1: Private, 9th Regiment, Veteran Reserve Corps, 1864
2: Captain, Invalid Corps, 1863
2a: Chasseur-pattern forage cap
3: Private, 1st Mounted Infantry, Indian Home Guard, 1864

MEDICAL DEPARTMENT AND RELATED SERVICES
1: Hospital steward, Medical Department, 1862
2: Medical surgeon with the rank of captain, 1861
2a: Medical Surgeon cap insignia
3: Private, Ambulance
Corps, 1864

F

CORPS OF ENGINEERS AND ORDNANCE DEPARTMENT
1: First lieutenant, Corps of Engineers, 1863
1a: "Turreted castle" insignia
1b: "Eagle and essayons" button
2: Private, Company of Sappers,
Miners, and Pontoniers, 1861
3: Ordnance sergeant, 1864

MILITARY TELEGRAPH SERVICE AND SIGNAL CORPS
1: Military telegrapher, Department of the Tennessee, 1864
2: Second Lieutenant, Signal Corps, 1864
3: Private, Signal Corps, 1864
3a: Signal Corps patch

THE INVALID/VETERAN RESERVE CORPS

Authorized by the War Department via General Orders No. 15 on April 28, 1863, the Invalid Corps was recruited mainly from partially disabled soldiers in general hospitals and convalescent camps in the various states. Modeled on those created in European armies, it was designed as an attempt to retain reasonably effective men in the service as staff or guards in Army hospitals.

Commanded by Provost Marshal General James B. Fry, the Invalid Corps was initially organized into 240 separate numbered companies. Between October 10, 1863, and February 24, 1864, these were reorganized into the 1st through 24th regiments, Invalid Corps, although about 188 companies remained unassigned to regiments. A regiment was normally composed of ten infantry companies, six in its 1st Battalion and four in the 2d Battalion. The ranks of 1st Battalion companies were filled with those who could handle a musket and undertake light marches. These men were used for guard duty on railroads, bridges, and government property, and guarding prisoners of war or drafted men. Those less physically able served in the 2d Battalion companies as clerks, cooks, or ancillary hospital nurses.

On May 15, 1863, General Orders No. 124 prescribed a uniform for enlisted men of the Invalid Corps consisting of a "Jacket. – Of sky-blue kersey, with dark blue trimmings, cut like the jacket for United States cavalry, to come well down on the loins and abdomen. Trowsers. – Present regulation, sky-blue. Forage cap. – Present regulation" (*PI*, May 21, 1863: 1:2).

FAR LEFT
Private Samuel F. McIntyre served in Co. B, 13th Massachusetts Infantry from June 1861 until August 5, 1862, after which he was listed as absent sick until September 17, 1863, when he was transferred to the Invalid Corps. Following reorganization of the Invalid Corps into the Veteran Reserve Corps, he joined Co. B, 21st Regiment, VRC, when it was formed on January 12, 1865. He wears the sky-blue kersey jacket with dark-blue trim and sky-blue trousers, adopted by the Invalid Corps on May 15, 1863, and holds a non-regulation straw hat. (Library of Congress LC-DIG-ppmsca-71526)

LEFT
Second Lieutenant Frank R. Rice, 2d Battalion, Invalid Corps, wears the officer's sky-blue uniform with dark-blue velvet collar and cuffs prescribed on June 11, 1863. Previously he had served in Co. F and Co. G, 1st Michigan Infantry. (Library of Congress LC-DIG-ppmsca-40721)

Two weeks later, on May 29, the "Army Clothing and Equipage Office" at the Schuylkill Arsenal began to request "Sealed Proposals" for sky-blue "Uniform Jackets" for the Invalid Corps (*PI*, May 30, 1863: 5:2). On June 11, officers were authorized to wear a

> Frock-coat. – Of sky-blue cloth, with dark blue velvet collar and cuffs; in all other respects according to the present pattern for officers of infantry. Shoulder straps. – According to present regulations, but worked on dark blue velvet. Pantaloons. – Of sky-blue cloth, with double stripe of dark-blue cloth down the outer seam, each stripe one-half inch wide, with a space between of three eighths of an inch. (*SG*, June 20, 1863: 2:7)

Regarding insignia, enlisted men of the Invalid Corps wore the brass infantry bugle on their cap tops or fronts, while officers wore the embroidered infantry bugle on cap fronts. By 1865, enlisted men in some companies had received regulation dark-blue frock and sack coats. Some officers objected to wearing sky-blue frock coats because it made them stand out from line units, and obtained dark-blue ones. Others adopted sky-blue jackets probably from cutting down frock coats, which they tended to wear open with sky-blue vests.

Companies of the 1st Battalion were issued with arms ranging from .69-caliber Springfield Model 1842 rifled muskets to Austrian, Prussian, and French smoothbore muskets, caliber .69 to .72. The Invalid Corps also carried a great many revolvers including Lefaucheux, Starr, and Savage patterns, which were mainly issued to personnel of its 2d battalions. Accouterments were regulation infantry pattern and included haversacks and knapsacks, which were issued as required. Men of the 2d battalions, and probably NCOs, were also issued with Model 1840 NCO swords.

When volunteer regimental bands were officially disbanded via General Orders No. 91 in July 1862, bands organized by the Invalid Corps supplemented those remaining at brigade level by providing music for hospitals, parades, and other special occasions. Stationed in Washington, DC, the 9th and 10th regiments, Invalid Corps, had both bands and drum corps and wore colorful non-regulation uniforms.

Unfortunately, the name Invalid Corps proved unpopular as "I.C." was jokingly referred to as "Inspected and Condemned," with reference to the term used by inspectors who condemned meat as not fit for human consumption, and on March 18, 1864, via General Orders No. 111 the Invalid Corps was redesignated the Veteran Reserve Corps (*ORs* 1900, Series 3, Vol. 4: 188).

Several Veteran Reserve Corps regiments saw action. On June 20, 1864, the 18th Regiment took part in the defense of White House, Virginia, against Confederate cavalry under Major General Wade Hampton. When the Confederate Second Corps, Army of Northern Virginia, commanded by Lieutenant General Jubal A. Early, attacked the Federal capital during July 11–12, 1864, the 9th Regiment was brought into action at Fort Stevens after the Confederates had pushed their picket line to within a short distance of the fortification and wounded several artillerymen. Ordered to charge, the 9th Regiment "drove the enemy some distance, and maintained a sharp skirmish until night, losing 5 killed and 7 severely wounded" (*ORs* 1900, Series 3, Vol. 5: 553).

Serving as a private in Co. F, 1st Colorado Cavalry, Joseph W. Aldrich was one of 24 men killed when his regiment attacked the Cheyenne/Arapaho encampment of Black Kettle at Sand Creek, Colorado Territory, on November 29, 1864. He wears die-struck Pattern 1858 brass dragoon/cavalry "crossed sabers" insignia on the front of his forage cap, with the company letter "F" above and the regimental number "1" below, according to 1861 Regulations. He wears a mounted service jacket and reinforced trousers, and is armed with a Sharps carbine and Model 1860 saber. (Denver Public Library, Western History Collection Z-517)

THE TERRITORIES

Organized on February 28, 1861, Colorado Territory recruited three regiments of cavalry, two regiments of infantry, and one light-artillery battery. All were occasionally clothed in regulation US Army uniforms, which were transported 600 miles by wagon to Denver from Fort Leavenworth, Kansas. Three battalions of cavalry were organized in Dakota Territory for local protection in 1862 and 1863. Raised by direct authority of the War Department, they were issued regulation US cavalry uniforms. One company of the 1st Battalion was armed with lances in 1864.

To replace the withdrawal of regular troops for the war effort back east, five infantry regiments were recruited in the territories of New Mexico and Arizona during 1861–62, one of which was mounted, plus one cavalry regiment. Having become a state on October 31, 1864, Nevada organized single battalions of infantry and cavalry while still a territory, while Nebraska Territory raised two regiments of cavalry, one of which was later converted to infantry. Most of these troops wore US Army regulation uniforms of either infantry or cavalry pattern when available. In the Southwest this was supplemented at times by locally sourced clothing such as bolero jackets or heavily trimmed trousers known as *calzoneras*.

Washington Territory organized only one regiment of infantry for Civil War service, mostly recruited in California due to distractions caused by a Gold Rush, strong Democrat support for the Confederacy, and trouble with Native Americans. Designated the 1st Volunteer Infantry, it wore regulation US infantry uniforms. With its local military encompassed by the Nauvoo Legion, none of the militia of the Mormon Utah Territory was directly clothed by the Federal Government, although some acquired US Army clothing via private sources.

THE US INDIAN HOME GUARD

Recruited among the Cherokee, Creek, Wichita, and Seminole peoples in response to Confederate efforts to gain support among the inhabitants of Indian Territory, the Indian Home Guard was a series of volunteer regiments under the leadership of Muscogee Creek Chief Opothleyahola. When organized in 1862 and 1863, the 1st, 2nd, and 3d Mounted regiments, Indian Home Guard, were under overall command of white officers, although leadership of individual companies was given to Native Americans. A 4th Regiment and a 5th Regiment failed to complete organization.

Unfamiliar with Army discipline or tactics, the enlisted men did not immediately become members of effective fighting units. Not immediately issued with uniforms, many wore ragged civilian clothing, but were described while on a march in 1862 as "decorated in war paint and feathers" (Britton 1922: 188).

Serving as interpreters between the white commanders and Native American enlisted men, the African Creeks and African Seminoles among their ranks were the first Black troops to be mustered into the Union Army, and the first to experience combat during the Indian Expedition into the Indian Territory in the summer of 1862. When Army clothing was issued at Fort Gibson in Oklahoma Territory during May 1864, the Native American personnel received the "Hancock Hat," while white officers wore the regulation headgear (Britton 1922: 226). Nearly all of the Native Americans were mounted on ponies.

This unidentified sergeant of the Indian Home Guard wears a four-button sack coat and has a bandolier pouch over his shoulder and a shell-bead necklace around his neck. The blanket he has wrapped around him possibly indicates his status among his people as well as his regiment. (Library of Congress LC-DIG-ppmsca-56933)

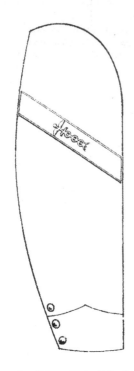

This detail from Plate 172 of the *Atlas to Accompany the Official Records of the Union and Confederate Armies 1861–1865* shows the caduceus sleeve insignia worn by hospital stewards of the Union Army. (Author's collection)

These chevrons were worn by a soldier assigned from the 1st Maine Heavy Artillery to serve as a hospital steward. (Military & Historical Image Bank CWi47ds)

THE MEDICAL DEPARTMENT AND RELATED SERVICES

At the outbreak of the Civil War, the personnel of the Medical Department of the US Army included surgeons, assistant surgeons, civilian physicians hired on contract, and hospital stewards. At any level of service, from regiment to corps, surgeons and assistant surgeons were considered members of the headquarters staff, and it was difficult to distinguish them from staff officers of equivalent rank in other departments.

The uniform of Army surgeons and assistant surgeons consisted of a dark-blue Pattern 1851 frock coat with gilt epaulets for full dress bearing in the crescent on the strap the silver letters "MS" within a gold embroidered laurel wreath. Surgeons' shoulder straps sometimes had the silver embroidered letters "MS" at the center, although this was not prescribed in regulations during the Civil War. Their hats and officer-pattern forage caps often bore a small non-regulation insignia at the front consisting of a gold bullion wreath and the silver letters "MS" embroidered on black velvet. Dark-blue trousers had a ⅛in.-wide buff welt in the outside seam. If worn, the most distinctive aspect of their dress was an emerald-green waist sash.

Usually only worn for dress occasions, the Model 1840 medical staff sword prescribed for surgeons and assistant surgeons had a straight blade, pineapple-shaped pommel, no knuckle guard, a specially molded grip bearing oak-leaf and acorn devices and a national eagle, and a scrolled quillon bearing two shields, the obverse having the letters "MS" in Old English script and the reverse plain. Sword-belt plates were of the pattern worn by general and staff officers.

Soldiers detailed to the hospital service as hospital stewards held the rank of NCO and ranked with ordnance sergeants. As a result of the Revised Army Regulations of 1861, they were also next above the first sergeant of a company. According to *The Hospital Steward's Manual*, published in 1862, hospital stewards were required to wear undress uniform when on duty in hospital, but full dress when attending muster and inspection. The latter was mostly the same pattern of uniform as that worn by NCOs of other branches of service, although the full-dress hat had a cord of buff and green with "US" in a wreath device at the front; the waist sash was scarlet, the dark-blue trousers had a 1½in.-wide crimson stripe, and they carried a sword of the NCO model. Rather than full NCO sleeve chevrons, the specialism of a hospital steward was indicated by a half-chevron of green edged with yellow worn on both arms. First authorized in 1851, this bore a caduceus device (often used as a symbol of medicine) consisting of the traditional symbol of the Greek god Hermes composed of two snakes winding around a winged staff.

On hospital duty, hospital stewards wore a frock coat or blouse open at the front to show a dark-blue vest, dark- or sky-blue trousers, but no belt or waist sash. The usual headgear consisted of an officer-pattern chasseur cap or black hat on which some wore a smaller version of the officer's non-regulation insignia.

During the early stages of the Civil War, most regiments organized their own provisional ambulance detachment or corps, and its officers, drivers, and stretcher-bearers wore the uniform of their regiment without

distinctive insignia. At the suggestion of Medical Director Charles S. Tripler, General Orders No. 20 was issued to the Army of the Potomac. It required that ten hospital attendants be appointed within each regiment, and that they, plus regimental bandsmen, should be drilled for one hour each day, except Sundays, by the regimental medical officer "in setting up and dismantling the hand-stretchers, litters, and ambulances; in handling men carefully; placing them upon the litters and ambulance beds; putting them into the ambulances, taking them out" (Barnes 1883: 935).

By early 1862 it became the practice to consolidate these detachments, although still provisional, under brigade or corps control so that they could serve more than their own regiments. The system remained haphazard, however, and control needed to be concentrated at higher levels of command and a permanent and more substantial organization had to be created.

In May 1862, the "Army Correspondent" of the *Chicago Daily Tribune* with the Army of the Mississippi, under Major General Henry W. Halleck, reported that a General Order had been issued to the effect that "all musicians, buglers, and drummers" in the brigade of Brigadier General John B. Palmer, First Division, Army of the Mississippi, were to serve as "the ambulance corps, under charge, in the field, of the chaplain, whose duty it is to carry off the wounded. They are designated by a green badge" (*CDT*, May 22, 1862: 2:3).

In August of that year, Dr. Jonathan Letterman, Medical Director for the Army of the Potomac, authorized Special Order No. 147 which created the Ambulance Corps. As a result, the Ambulance Corps in each corps was commanded by a captain; a first lieutenant commanded that for a division, a second lieutenant for a brigade, and a sergeant for a regiment.

Worn by an unknown soldier attached to the Ambulance Corps, this forage cap has the green band adopted in August 1862. (Military & Historical Image Bank CWc56d)

Each regiment, no matter which branch of service, had one transport cart and five ambulances assigned to it; each battery of artillery had one ambulance; and each corps headquarters had two ambulances. Every ambulance was manned by one private as a driver and two as stretcher-bearers (Barnes 1883: 936).

Although still detailed from the ranks, enlisted men now wore distinctive insignia, which was prescribed as "for privates, a green band, two inches broad, around the cap, a green half-chevron, two inches broad, on each arm above the elbow …" They were also to be "armed with revolvers." NCOs were "to wear the same band around the cap as the privates, chevrons two inches broad, and green, with point toward the shoulder, on each arm above the elbow" (Barnes 1883: 937). During August 1863, the Army of the Potomac issued revised regulations for insignia for its Ambulance Corps, which stipulated that sergeants should wear "a green band, one and a quarter inches broad, around the cap, and chevrons of the same material, with the point toward the shoulder, on each arm above the elbow. For privates, by a band, the same as for sergeants, around the cap, and a half-chevron of the same material on each arm above the elbow" (Barnes 1883: 940).

When an Ambulance Corps was instituted in the Army of the Cumberland in January 1864 a second lieutenant in charge of the brigade train commanded two sergeants, while the number of privates and drivers remained the same as in the Army of the Potomac. At the same time, Major General George H. Thomas copied Letterman's system as developed by 1863 and, via General Orders No. 1, ordered the Ambulance Corps in the Department of the Cumberland to wear 1¼in. broad green bands around their caps and arms (*General Orders* 1865: 6).

Green was not the only color of insignia used to identify those detailed to the Ambulance Corps. On December 30, 1862, Major General John G. Foster, commanding the XVIII Corps at New Bern, North Carolina, ordered that "the uniform or distinctive badge of this corps [ambulance] shall be, for private and NCOs, a broad red band around the cap with a knot upon the right side, and a red band, one inch wide, above the elbow upon each arm" (*ORs* 1898, Series 1, Vol. 3: 81).

On March 30, 1863, Major General Ulysses S. Grant endorsed white insignia for the Department of the Tennessee with General Orders No. 22, in which he ordered that "enlisted men detailed to attend ambulances … will wear a white badge on the left arm above the elbow, the same to be provided by the Medical Department" (Barnes 1883: 938). As late as the battle of Cold Harbor in May–June 1864, musician George T. Ulmer, Co. H, 8th Maine Infantry, described how men assigned to "the stretcher corps" wore a "little white cloth" around their arms (Ulmer 1892: 40).

The establishment of a uniform Ambulance Corps system for the Union Army was not accomplished until March 1864, when all employed or detailed Ambulance Corps men and "ambulances, medicine and other wagons, horses, mules, harness, and other fixtures" came under the control of the medical director of the army to which each corps belonged (Barnes 1883: 941).

THE CORPS OF ENGINEERS

At the beginning of the Civil War the Corps of Engineers consisted of 43 officers plus a Company of Sappers, Miners, and Pontoniers, which had been authorized via General Orders No. 14 and established on May 15, 1846. By 1861 the dress of engineer officers was distinguished by "eagle and essayons" coat buttons and a "turreted castle" hat insignia as described under staff officers.

The dress for engineer enlisted men consisted of a Pattern 1858 frock coat with collar and cuffs edged with yellow cord; and sky-blue trousers with yellow seam stripes indicating rank for sergeants and corporals. Hats were looped up on the left side with a Pattern 1858 brass "eagle" plate as per other foot troops, with a yellow worsted hat cord and a Pattern 1858 brass "turreted castle" and company letter at the front of the crown. The first to receive the Pattern 1858 forage cap, engineer troops had a "turreted castle" insignia at the front or on top of their headgear.

For fatigue purposes, engineer enlisted men wore white cotton canvas overalls described as "one garment to cover the whole of the body below the waist, the breast, the shoulders and the arms; sleeves loose, to allow a free play of the arms, with narrow wristband buttoning with one button; overalls to fasten at the neck behind with two buttons, and at the waist behind with buckle and tongue" (*Regulations* 1861: 16).

On January 18, 1861, the Company of Sappers, Miners, and Pontoniers, commanded by First Lieutenant James C. Duane (who later served as Chief Engineer of the Army of the Potomac 1863–65), numbering 64 officers and men, was ordered to Washington, DC, to serve as infantry guarding the public buildings, stores, and arsenals during the secessionist crisis. It also formed part of the escort for President Lincoln at his first inauguration on March 4, 1861. On arrival at the Capitol on January 21, this company wore a fatigue dress consisting of a blue/gray jacket, dark-blue trousers, and Pattern 1857 forage caps with rainproof covers (*FLIN*, February 9, 1861: 5). According to a newspaper report they were armed with rifles and saber bayonets (*NYH*, January 21, 1861: 1:2).

On August 3, 1861, Congress authorized three additional engineer companies and six more lieutenants for the Corps of Engineers, and the original company was redesignated Co. A. Although the official name adopted was the Battalion of Sappers, Miners, and Pontoniers, it was referred to as the US Engineer Battalion in most orders and correspondence. Each company of the battalion was to consist of 150 enlisted men, including ten sergeants, ten corporals, a drummer and fifer, 64 privates first class or artificers, and 64 privates second class. This set the authorized strength of the Corps of Engineers at 49 officers and 550 enlisted men. An Act of August 6, 1861, added two lieutenant colonels and four majors (Thienel 1955: 36).

Co. B was recruited in Portland, Maine, and Co. C in Boston, Massachusetts. During the Fall of 1861, the Engineer Battalion became the nucleus for the newly organized Volunteer Engineer Brigade of the Army of the Potomac. By July 1, 1862, however, the battalion numbered only 276 men on the rolls. During November 1862, Co. D was organized from drafts from the other three companies. Pattern 1858 sack coats and sky-blue trousers were worn by the whole battalion throughout the Civil War.

On June 20, 1864, Congress established the position of sergeant major in the Battalion of Sappers, Miners, and Pontoniers, with pay of $36 per month. Nearly three years later, on February 21, 1867, the commander of the battalion designated Frederick W. Gerber as permanent sergeant major, making him the Corps of Engineers' senior enlisted man and battalion adjutant. Having served in the 1st Engineer Battalion during the Mexican–American War, Gerber had a service record that made him a natural choice for the position. He wears the "turreted castle" insignia on his hat and below his sleeve chevrons are service stripes, each of which indicates a three-year period of service. He is armed with a Model 1840 NCO sword. (Courtesy of the Office of History, HQ, US Army Corps of Engineers)

ORDNANCE SERGEANTS AND ENLISTED MEN

This ordnance sergeant has a regulation Pattern 1851 brass "flaming bomb" insignia and crimson cord on his hat. Besides the sleeve chevrons, his rank is indicated by 1½in.-wide crimson welts on his trousers. (National Gallery of Art, Robert B. Menschel Fund and the Vital Projects Fund: Acc. No. 2009.75.5)

Besides officers, the Ordnance Department included ordnance sergeants who served as caretakers of ordnance and other stores at military installations, and supervised civilian employees of the various Federal arsenals and armories, the number of which increased from 1,000 to 9,000 by war's end (Rubis 2022: website). The rank of ordnance sergeant was the most senior NCO grade in the Ordnance Department and one that could be earned only after many years of service.

From about May 1854, ordnance sergeants wore for dress the uniform coat trimmed with crimson lace on the collar and cuffs, and noncommissioned staff brass shoulder scales. Trousers were dark blue, later sky blue, with 1½in.-wide crimson lace on the outer seam. The Pattern 1858 hat had a Pattern 1851 brass "flaming bomb" insignia at the front and crimson cord. Rank was displayed by three crimson silk chevrons and a star. A red worsted sash was worn under a plain black leather sword belt fastened by a Pattern 1851 rectangular "eagle" plate and supporting a Model 1840 NCO sword in a sliding frog. Most Ordnance Department privates wore the same full dress minus rank insignia, and enlisted-pattern shoulder scales and plain trousers.

Fatigue clothing for all enlisted men included a dark-blue jacket trimmed with crimson; when not available, such garments were supplemented by cutting the skirts of a frock coat. Sack coats and forage caps with a "flaming bomb" insignia on the top were also worn for undress. Ordnance men were armed and equipped as infantry.

Military storekeepers employed by the Ordnance Department, of whom there were 15 in 1861, were given the rank and pay as major or captain of cavalry. They were responsible for stores in an arsenal and could serve as paymasters. The dress regulation of military storekeepers since 1851 had been a "citizen's frockcoat of blue cloth, with buttons of the department … round black hat; pantaloons and vest, plain, white or dark blue; cravat or stock, black" (*Regulations* 1851: 13).

THE MILITARY TELEGRAPH SERVICE

The Military Telegraph Service was organized in November 1861 to operate all electrical communication for the Union Army. Its personnel were mainly civilians and were composed of skilled telegraphers and construction crews who erected lines of communication. These individuals were nominally employees of the Quartermaster Department but in reality were under direct control of the Superintendent of the Military Telegraph Service, Colonel Anson Stager, or Secretary of War Stanton, who stressed they were not subject to orders of field commanders. As a result, no uniform was prescribed by the War Department for military telegraph personnel.

This independent status was resented by several commanders, including Grant and Sherman, and led to conflict with the War Department over the Military Telegraph Service. It was also a matter

of concern for telegraphers and crews. Often working close to enemy territory and subject to raids, their civilian clothing placed them in grave danger of being captured. This was particularly the case in the Midwest along the valleys of the Cumberland and the Tennessee rivers, where long lines of communication were required. Indeed, on October 28, 1863, Assistant Superintendent Captain Samuel Bruch reported from his headquarters at Louisville, Kentucky, to Stager: "A number of operators; in Tennessee and Kentucky were captured and paroled and robbed of their money, watches, and other articles of value by the prowling bands of guerrillas who infested every part of the country" (*OR*, Series 1, Vol. 52: 480).

Eventually on March 26, 1864, Major General George H. Thomas authorized General Orders No. 51, which permitted telegraph operators within the Department of the Cumberland to wear an undress uniform consisting of a dark-blue blouse, or sack coat; dark-blue trousers with a ⅛in.-wide silver cord along the outer seam; buff, white, or blue vest; officer-pattern forage cap without distinctive mark or ornament; and with all buttons of the "General Service" pattern. On July 5, 1864, Major General James B. McPherson, commanding the Department of the Tennessee, issued a similar order, except that there was to be a narrow silver cord around the cap band (Lord 1970: 81).

THE SIGNAL CORPS

For the first three years of the Civil War, signal communications were handled on an experimental basis by acting signal officers who were

Second Lieutenant
William F. Barrett, Co. C,
27th Massachusetts Infantry,
was detached from his unit to
serve with the Signal Corps
as an acting signal officer on
December 27, 1861, by order
of Major General Ambrose E.
Burnside. Barrett was honorably
discharged from the volunteer
service while at the Signal
Corps Camp of Instruction on
Red Hill, Georgetown, DC, on
June 3, 1863, and appointed in
the Regular Army as a second
lieutenant of the Signal Corps
on the same date. This *carte de
visite* was produced in Nashville,
Tennessee, by photographer
Theodore M. Schleier between
April and July 1864. He wears
a cloth patch on the front of his
cap bearing the "crossed signal
flags" insignia of the Signal
Corps, and has narrow, plain
shoulder straps on his officer-
pattern sack coat. (Library of
Congress LC-DIG-ppmsca-71930)

subalterns of volunteer regiments specially detailed for the purpose. A Signal Corps was finally created via the Act of March 3, 1863, which authorized the detailing of officers ranging from colonel to lieutenant and enlisted men from sergeant to private.

Operating in small units attached to the higher headquarters, officers were responsible for encoding and decoding signals, while enlisted men would wave the flag and observe incoming messages. All personal were mounted, which enabled them to move quickly from place to place. Their equipment consisted of several sizes of flags, torches or signal lights for night signaling, and telescopes, which could be quickly packed up and transported on horseback. The average distance that signals were sent and received was 8–15 miles, depending on weather conditions.

Major Albert J. Myer, who organized the Signal Corps attached to the Army of Northeastern Virginia in 1861, was authorized on June 15 of that year to wear the uniform of a major of the General Staff. Acting signal officers detailed to him wore the uniform of their original corps. On July 22, 1864, Major William J.L. Nicodemus, commanding the Signal Corps Camp of Instruction on Red Hill, Georgetown, DC, sent a request to the Adjutant General for general orders to be issued prescribing a uniform for the Signal Corps. This request was turned down with the exception of cloth insignia approved by General Orders No. 36 on August 22, 1864, which permitted a distinctive device consisting of "crossed flags" to be worn by officers on their hats and caps and the men on their sleeves. The device for officers consisted of

a gold embroidered wreath … on black velvet ground, encircling crossed signal flags, with lighted torch, and supported by the letters "U.S." in silver old English characters. *Color of flags:* one red, with white center; the other white, with red center. *Size of flag:* three-eighths of an inch square; size of center, one-eighth of an inch square; length of staff, one and one-sixteenth inches. (Todd 1977: 401)

That for enlisted men was composed of

Crossed signal flags, red and white, on dark blue cloth. *Size of Flags:* three-fourths of an inch square; center, one-quarter of an inch square; length of staff, three inches. Sergeants will wear the designation of the corps placed in the angle of the chevron upon the left sleeve. Privates will wear the designation of the corps in the same position on the left sleeve as the chevron of sergeants. (Todd 1977: 401)

Although prescribed to be worn on the left sleeve by enlisted men, the "crossed signal flags" insignia was in practice, and according to photographic evidence, worn on the right sleeve or both.

Further evidence also indicates that a commonly accepted uniform worn by Signal Corps enlisted men early in the Civil War was the mounted service jacket and trousers, the former being without branch service lace. Detached from Co. A, 45th Massachusetts Infantry, to join the Signal Service on December 4, 1862, Private George A. Estabrook recalled, "For arms we had Colt's revolvers. I don't think I ever had occasion to fire mine. For uniform, cavalry jackets, as well as our usual regimentals, and cavalry trousers, with reinforced seats" (Mann 1908: 95).

SELECT BIBLIOGRAPHY

Barnes, Joseph K. *et al.* (1883). *The Medical and Surgical History of the War of the Rebellion*, Part 3, Vol. 2, "Surgical History." Washington, DC: Government Printing Office.

Bates, David H. (1907). *Lincoln in the Telegraph Office: Recollections of the United States Military Telegraph Corps during the Civil War*. New York, NY: D. Appleton-Century Company Inc.

Britton, Wiley (1922). *The Union Indian Brigade in the Civil War.* Kansas City, MO: Franklin Hudson Publishing Co.

Coates, Earl J., & John D. McAulay (1996). *Civil War Sharps Carbines & Rifles*. Gettysburg, PA: Thomas Publications.

Coker, Kathy R. & Carol E. Stokes (1994). *A Concise History of the U.S. Army Signal Corps*. Fort Gordon, GA: US Army Signal Center.

Davis, Major General George W. (1880–1901). *The War of the Rebellion: a Compilation of the Official Records of the Union and Confederate Armies*. (*ORs*) Washington, DC: Government Printing Office.

Eicher, John H. & David J. Eicher (2001). *Civil War High Commands*. Stanford, CA: Stanford University Press.

Elting, Lieutenant Colonel John R. (1954). "The United States Sharpshooters," *Military Collector and Historian*, Vol. VI, No. 3 (September): 57–61.

Gaede, F.C. (1999). "A Model of 1858 Forage Cap," *Military Collector and Historian*, Vol. 51, No. 2 (Summer): 66–69.

Gaede, F.C. (2022). "Ponchos and Waterproof Blankets During the Civil War," *Military Images*, Vol. 40, No. 2 (Spring): 70–74.

General Orders affecting the Volunteer Force, 1864 (1865). Washington, DC: Government Printing Office.

General Orders, Department of the Cumberland, 1864 (1865). Washington, DC: Government Printing Office.

Ginn, Richard V.N. (1997). *The History of the U.S. Army Medical Service Corps*. United States Army. Washington, DC: Office of the Surgeon General and Center of Military History, US Army.

Heitman, Francis B. (1903). *Historical Register and Dictionary of the United States Army*, Vol. 1. Washington, DC: Government Printing Office.

Hewett, Janet B. (ed.) (1998). *Supplement to the Official Records of the Union and Confederate Armies*, Part II, Vol. 79. Wilmington, NC: Broadfoot Publishing Co.

Howell, Edgar M. (1975). *United States Army Headgear 1855–1902. Catalog of United States Army Uniforms in the Collections of the Smithsonian Institution, II*. Washington, DC: Smithsonian Institution.

Letterman, Jonathan (1866). *Medical Recollections of the Army of the Potomac*. New York, NY: D. Appleton & Co.

Lord, Francis A. (1970). *Uniforms of the Civil War*. Mineola, NY: Dover Publications, Inc.

Mann, Albert W. (1908). *History of the Forty-Fifth Regiment Massachusetts Volunteer Militia*. Jamaica Plain, MA: Brookside Print.

McAulay, John D. (1996). *Carbines of the U.S. Cavalry 1861–1865*. Lincoln, RI: Andrew Mowbray Publishers.

McAulay, John D. (2003). *Rifles of the U.S. Army 1861–1906*. Lincoln, RI: Andrew Mowbray Publishers.

McKee, Paul (1995). "Notes on the Federal Issue Sack Coat," *Military Collector & Historian*, Vol. 47, No. 2 (Summer): 50–59.

Myer, Albert J. (1866). *A Manual of Signals for the Use of Signal Officers in the Field*. New York, NY: D. Van Nostrand, 192 Broadway.

Newell, Clayton R. (2014). *The Regular Army Before the Civil War*. Washington, DC: Center of Military History, United States Army (PDF).

Ripley, Lieutenant Colonel Wm. Y.W. (1883). *The Vermont Riflemen in the War for the Union, 1861–1865. A History of Company F, First United States Sharp Shooters*. Rutland, VT: Tuttle & Co.

Rodenbough, Theo F. (1875). *From Everglade to Cañon with the Second Dragoons*. New York, NY: D. Van Nostram.

Rubis, Karl (2022). "History of Ordnance in America," https://goordnance.army.mil/history/ordhistory.html

Stevens, Captain Charles Augustus (1892). *Berdan's United States Sharpshooters in the Army of the Potomac 1861–1865*. St. Paul, MN: The Price-McGill Co.

Springer, George F. (1885). *Concise History of the Camp and Field Life of the 122d Regiment, Penn'a Volunteers*. Lancaster, PA: The New Era Steam Book Print.

Thienel, Phillip M. (1955). "Engineers in the Union Army, 1861–1865," *The Military Engineer*, Vol. 47, No. 315 (January–February): 36–41.

Todd, F.P. (1974). *American Military Equipage 1851–1872*. Volume I. Providence, RI: The Company of Military Historians.

Todd, F.P. (1977). *American Military Equipage 1851–1872*. Volume II. Providence, RI: The Company of Military Historians.

Ulmer, George T. (1892). *Adventures and Reminiscences of a Volunteer, or a Drummer Boy from Maine*. Washington, DC: privately published.

US War Department (1851). *Regulations for the Uniform & Dress of the Army of the United States. June 1851*. Philadelphia, PA: William H. Horstmann & Sons.

US War Department (1861). *Regulations for the Uniform and Dress of the Army of the United States. 1861*. Washington, DC: George W. Bowman, Public Printer.

US War Department (1863). *Revised United States Army Regulations of 1861* (1863). Washington, DC: Government Printing Office.

Wagner, Margaret E., Gary W. Gallagher, and Paul Finkelman (2002). *The Library of Congress Civil War Desk Reference*. New York, NY: Simon & Schuster.

Wilson, Mark R. (2006). *The Business of Civil War: Military Mobilization and the State, 1861–1865*. Baltimore, MD: Johns Hopkins University Press.

Newspapers

Belmont Chronicle, Belmont, OH (*BC*); *Chicago Daily Tribune*, Chicago, IL (*CDT*); *Daily Green Mountain Freeman*, Montpelier, VT (*DGMF*); *Detroit Free Press*, Detroit, MI (*DFP*); *Fall River Daily Evening News*, Fall River, MA (*FRDEN*); *Frank Leslie's Illustrated Newspaper*, New York, NY (*FLIN*); *Hartford Courant*, Hartford, CT (*HC*); *Military Gazette*, Albany, NY (*MG*); *New York Herald*, New York, NY (*NYH*); *New York Tribune*, New York, NY (*NYT*); *Philadelphia Inquirer*, Philadelphia, PA (*PI*); *Pittsfield Sun*, Pittsfield, MA (*PS*); *Public Ledger*, Philadelphia, PA (*PL*); *Sunbury Gazette*, Sunbury, PA (*SG*); *Vermont Standard*, Woodstock, VT (*VS*).

PLATE COMMENTARIES

A: INFANTRY

(1) Infantry colonel, 1861

Based on an image of Colonel Erasmus D. Keyes, 11th Infantry, while he served briefly on the staff of the Governor of New York, Edwin D. Morgan, in 1861, this infantry officer wears a *chapeau de bras*, or cocked hat, with three black ostrich feathers authorized for generals and staff officers via General Orders No. 3, dated March 24, 1858. His Pattern 1851 officer's frock coat has two rows of seven large "infantry I" buttons (1a) at the front and three small "infantry I" buttons on the underside of each cuff. His dress epaulets have the regimental number "11" embroidered in gold on a sky-blue ground within the brass crescent, and a silver embroidered "spread eagle" at the center of the strap. His dark-blue trousers have a ⅛in.-wide sky-blue welt in the outside seams in line with regulations for infantry. A Pattern 1851 officer's belt plate (1b) fastens his sword belt, underneath which is a crimson silk net waist sash. He carries a Model 1850 foot officer's sword.

(2) Company musician, 2d Infantry, 1862

He wears a Pattern 1858 forage cap and musician's frock coat with sky-blue "herringbone" pattern lace on the chest, and trim of the same color on the collar and cuffs. All buttons are "General Service" pattern. He also wears plain sky-blue kersey Pattern 1861 dismounted trousers. Footwear consists of ankle-high brogans with a smooth exterior of blackened leather, brown cord ties, wooden-pegged soles, and metal-pegged heels. His NCO waist belt has a Pattern 1851 enlisted "eagle" plate, and a shoulder belt with Pattern 1826 "eagle" plate supports a Model 1840 musician's sword in a leather frog and scabbard. His snare drum bears the standard interpretation of the coat of arms of the United States, and is supported by a canvas sling with brass drumstick holder attached.

(3) Corporal, 14th Infantry, 1864

This corporal has a waterproof cover on his forage cap and wears a flannel sack coat with four large "General Service" buttons at the front and sky-blue worsted chevrons indicating his rank and branch of service. His sky-blue kersey Pattern 1861 dismounted trousers have 1½in.-wide dark-blue worsted welts on the outer seams. He is armed with a Springfield rifled musket with fixed bayonet, with a brown leather sling attached, and a Model 1840 NCO sword in a leather scabbard. His accouterments consist of an NCO waist belt on which is slid a Pattern 1864 cartridge box with embossed "US" in an oval on the flap, and a Pattern 1855 Allegheny Arsenal cap pouch with "shield" front. He also carries a Philadelphia Depot-made oblate spheroid Pattern 1858 tin canteen with jean cloth cover, pewter spout, and leather strap; a black-painted canvas haversack with single flap and shoulder strap of the same material; and a non-rigid black waterproofed canvas knapsack with black leather straps and brass rivets, on top of which is secured a brown wool blanket roll.

B: ARTILLERY

(1) Captain, light-artillery company, 2d Artillery, 1864

This officer has a Pattern 1858 "crossed cannon" insignia with the regimental number "2" above the intersection attached to the crown of his Burnside-pattern slouch hat. Two black ostrich feathers are fixed on the side via a black silk cockade secured by a small artillery "eagle A" button. Attached to the turned-up brim is a Pattern 1858 officer's hat "eagle" insignia with a bullion embroidered eagle on a black velvet ground. His Pattern 1860 undress jacket is trimmed with scarlet around the collar, and has nine large artillery "eagle A" buttons at its front and three small buttons of the same pattern on the under seam of each cuff. The Russian knots (1a) on his shoulders have three gold cords as prescribed for company-grade officers. His mounted service trousers have a reinforced seat and inner leg, and a ½in.-wide scarlet welt let into the outer seams. Around his waist is a brown leather sword belt fastened with a Pattern 1851 officer's belt plate, underneath which is a crimson silk net waist sash. He carries a Model 1840 light-artillery saber.

(2) Bugler, light-artillery company, 5th Artillery, 1863

The Pattern 1858 cap worn by this bugler has a Pattern 1858 artillery "crossed cannon" insignia on its top with a brass regimental number "5" above. His Pattern 1854 musician's jacket has scarlet "herringbone" tape at the front, and scarlet trim on the collar and cuffs. All his buttons are "General Service" pattern. Enlisted man's brass shoulder scales adorn his shoulders. His plain sky-blue kersey trousers have a reinforced seat and inner leg for mounted troops. His brown leather Pattern 1851 enlisted cavalry belt has an enlisted man's-pattern "eagle" plate, and shoulder strap and hangers to help carry the weight of his Model 1840 light-artillery saber. He is also armed with a Colt Model 1851 Navy Revolver in a black leather holster. Accouterments consist of a Watervliet Arsenal cap pouch and pistol cartridge box. His bugle is suspended from his shoulder via its scarlet worsted cord.

(3) Sergeant, Battery E, 1st Artillery, 1861

Depicted in full dress, this artillery sergeant wears a Pattern 1858 hat with single ostrich feather plume, scarlet worsted cord with tassels, Pattern 1858 enlisted artillery insignia (3a) with company letter and regimental number above, and "eagle" hat insignia attached to the looped-up brim. His Pattern 1858 frock coat is trimmed with scarlet on the collar and cuffs. He has NCO shoulder scales, and all his buttons are "General Service" pattern. His sky-blue kersey dismounted service trousers have 1½in.-wide scarlet welts in the side seams. He is armed with a Springfield Model 1855 rifle musket minus sling, and a Model 1832 Foot Artillery sword attached via a frog to his waist belt. Accouterments include a Pattern 1857 cartridge box and an Allegheny Arsenal cap pouch with "shield" front.

C: DRAGOONS, MOUNTED RIFLEMEN, AND CAVALRY

(1) Private, 2d Dragoons, 1862

The Pattern 1861 forage cap worn by this dragoon private has a stamped-metal Pattern 1858 dragoon/cavalry "crossed sabers" insignia attached to its top. His Pattern 1854 uniform jacket is bound with orange lace around the collar, cuffs, and back seams by 12 small "General Service" buttons at the front and two on each cuff. The standing collar has two orange false buttonholes terminating in buttons of the same pattern on each side. He also wears enlisted man's brass shoulder scales. His plain enlisted man's trousers have a reinforced seat and inner leg for mounted troops, and his boots are privately purchased. He is armed with a Model 1840 cavalry saber and a .52-caliber Sharps Model 1853 breech-loading carbine. Some troopers also carried one or more revolvers. Equipment consists of a Pattern 1851 enlisted man's cavalry belt with "eagle" plate, and hangers to accommodate his saber scabbard; an Allegheny Arsenal-made cap pouch; and a carbine cartridge box. His horse has a Pattern 1859 McClellan saddle over a US-issued dragoon wool blanket with orange stripe.

(2) Private, Regiment of Mounted Riflemen, 1861

Depicted in full dress, this mounted rifleman wears a Pattern 1858 hat with green wool cord and tassels, single black ostrich feather, and enlisted man's die-struck brass trumpet at the front, above which is the company letter "B." His Pattern 1854 mounted service jacket has emerald-green trim around the collar, edges, and cuffs, and has 12 small "General Service" buttons at the front and two at each cuff opening. His trousers have a reinforced seat and inner leg for mounted troops and he wears boots with spurs. He is armed with a .58-caliber Model 1841 rifle. Accouterments consist of a Pattern 1855 rifle cartridge box, Allegheny Arsenal-made cap pouch, Pattern 1858 canteen with brown cloth cover, and painted cloth haversack.

(3) First Lieutenant, 2d Cavalry, 1864

Loading his Colt Navy revolver, this cavalry officer serving as an aide-de-camp wears a Burnside-pattern slouch hat with a Pattern 1858 "crossed sabers" insignia and the regimental number "2" above, officer's "eagle" hat insignia on the looped-up brim, two ostrich feathers attached via a small silk cockade with a "cavalry C" button at its center, and black and gold bullion cord. Completely edged and trimmed in custom black lace, his privately purchased jacket is based on a regulation stable jacket, and has nine gilt "General Staff" buttons (3a) at the front. His shoulder straps are "Smith's Patent" with a double imitation embroidery border over a yellow background and brass lieutenant's bars. His mounted service trousers have a ⅛in.-wide yellow welt in the outer seams. His top-boots are also privately purchased. Other weaponry consists of a Model 1860 officer's cavalry saber, and accouterments include a Pattern 1861 cavalry saber belt with a Model 1851 brass belt plate, leather revolver holster, cap pouch, and pistol cartridge box.

D: US COLORED TROOPS AND US SHARPSHOOTERS

(1) Private, 12th Infantry, USCT, 1864

This African American private wears a Pattern 1861 forage cap with a stamped-brass infantry horn (1a) on top and the company letter "E" above. His Pattern 1858 frock coat has nine large "General Service" buttons down the front and two small ones on each cuff, and has sky-blue trim. He also wears enlisted man's brass shoulder scales, white dress gloves, and sky-blue kersey Pattern 1861 trousers. He is armed with a Pattern 1853 Enfield rifle musket with a triangular socket bayonet. His accouterments consist of a Pattern 1839 belt and plate, cap pouch, and a Pattern 1864 cartridge box with embossed "US" on the outer flap on his shoulder belt with a Pattern 1826 "eagle" plate (1b).

(2) Private, 1st USSS, 1862

Both the "Havelock" hat and overcoat worn by this United States Sharpshooters private were made by the Seamless Clothing Manufacturing Company of New York. Designed by Jonathan F. Whipple in July 1861, the cap had a visor at the front and flaps that protected the back and sides of the

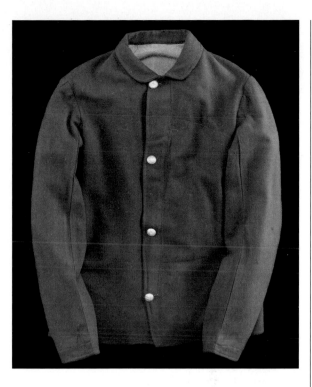

This Pattern 1858 sack coat was made under contract for the New York Clothing Depot by John T. Martin of New York City. Machine-sewn, it has four "General Service" eagle buttons on its front. The cuffs are plain and an inside breast pocket is sewn in the lining on the left side. The lining of the right sleeve has three stamps: "J.T. Martin, Feby 4 65," indicating date of inspection; "3," giving the sack coat's size; and "Jos. Jones, US Inspector, NY," naming the government inspector. (Smithsonian Institution NMAH 64127)

wearer's neck. Made of Austrian-gray felt, his overcoat is edged with green around the collar, cape, lower pocket flaps, and coat edges, and has five non-reflective hard rubber "General Service"-pattern buttons (2a), produced by the Novelty Rubber Company of New York, down its front and six smaller ones on its cape. His early-issue trousers are plain sky-blue kersey Pattern 1861, and his russet leather leggings are fastened by eight buckles and straps. He is armed with a Colt Model 1855 revolving rifle, and his equipment consists of a Pattern 1839 shoulder belt and Pattern 1855 cartridge box with plates removed. A cap pouch and Pattern 1855 bayonet in a scabbard are slid on to his waist belt, which has a Pattern 1839 oval "US" plate.

(3) Sergeant, 2d USSS, 1863

The headgear for this United States Sharpshooters sergeant consists of a forest-green Pattern 1861 forage cap with black ostrich feather plume. The blackened brass company letter "H" and regimental number "2" are affixed to its top. His forest-green Pattern 1858 frock coat is trimmed with emerald green on the collar and cuffs, and has nine large hard rubber "General Service" buttons at the front and two small ones on each cuff. His dark-green velvet chevrons are privately purchased. His matching trousers have 1½in.-wide sky-blue worsted welts on the outer seams. He is loading his Sharps

New Model 1859 breech-loading rifle with double-set trigger and shortened barrel, which has a scope mounted. His equipment includes a waist belt with a blackened Pattern 1839 "US" plate, on which is slid an Allegheny Arsenal cap pouch, cartridge box with plain outer flap, and bayonet in a scabbard. His hard-frame, calf hide-covered sergeant's Prussian-pattern knapsack has attached to it a gray blanket roll, hemp rope for climbing trees, and bronzed tin mess kit. He also carries a Philadelphia Depot oblate spheroid Pattern 1858 tin canteen with jean cloth cover, and a black-painted canvas haversack.

E: INVALID/VETERAN RESERVE CORPS AND US INDIAN HOME GUARD

(1) Private, 9th Regiment, Veteran Reserve Corps, 1864
This corporal wears a Pattern 1861 forage cap with infantry horn and regimental number at the front and a sky-blue kersey, polka-skirted jacket with dark-blue trim on the collar, shoulder straps, cuffs, and jacket edges. All buttons are small-size "General Staff" pattern. His sky-blue kersey Pattern 1861 dismounted service trousers have a ½in.-wide dark-blue welt in the outer seams. He is armed with a Springfield Model 1864 rifled musket and a socket bayonet in a scabbard. His equipment includes a Pattern 1839 belt and plate with cap pouch and a Pattern 1864 cartridge box with embossed "US" on the outer flap. He has a black-painted haversack, and his Pattern 1858 canteen with gray canvas cover is of the type supplied by makers to the New York Clothing Depot. On his back is a Pattern 1853/55 double-bag knapsack of black-painted canvas.

(2) Captain, Invalid Corps, 1863
This Invalid Corps officer wears a chasseur-pattern forage cap (**2a**) with black braid forming a quatrefoil loop on its top. His sky-blue Pattern 1851 frock coat has a dark-blue velvet collar and cuffs, and his captain's shoulder straps have a dark-blue velvet ground. His sky-blue trousers have a double welt of dark-blue cloth down the outer seams, each welt being ½in. wide, with a space between of ⅜in. He carries a Model 1850 foot officer's sword with gold bullion sword knot. A Pattern 1851 officer's belt plate fastens his black leather sword belt. As "Officer of the Day," he wears his crimson silk net sash under his belt and over his right shoulder. He has a Colt Army revolver in a black leather holster, Allegheny Arsenal cap pouch, and leather pistol cartridge box on his waist belt.

(3) Private, Indian Home Guard, 1864
This mounted private of the Indian Home Guard has eagle feathers attached to his black felt slouch hat, and wears an ill-fitting dark-blue Pattern 1854 frock coat with sky-blue trim around the collar and cuffs. All of the frock-coat buttons are "General Service" pattern. He wears Cherokee Tellico Plains beads around his neck. His sky-blue kersey Pattern 1861 dismounted trousers are tucked into fringed buckskin leggings, which are tied below the knee with beaded strands of red wool "strouding." Footwear consists of Cherokee beaded moccasins. He holds a Liége-made Model 1859 French short rifle over his saddle and has a Model 1842 saber bayonet with brass hilt and iron guard in a scabbard attached via a frog to his waist belt. His accouterments consist of a Pattern 1864 cartridge box, Pattern 1855 Allegheny Arsenal cap pouch, Philadelphia Depot oblate spheroid Pattern 1858 tin canteen with jean cloth cover, and black-painted canvas haversack. Horse equipment is composed of a war bridle consisting of a piece of rope with a small metal ring on each end that attaches to leather reins, and a brown leather saddle with off-white patterned saddle blanket.

F: MEDICAL DEPARTMENT AND RELATED SERVICES

(1) Hospital steward, Medical Department, 1862
On hospital duty, this steward carries a medical tin pannier containing linens, bandages, dressings, and medicine bottles. His chasseur-pattern forage cap has a small, rounder version of the non-regulation medical officer's "MS" in wreath insignia at the front. Trimmed with sky blue, his Pattern 1858 frock coat has "General Service" buttons, and is worn open to show his vest and non-regulation shirt. Ranked the same as an ordnance sergeant, he has green half-chevrons edged with yellow and bearing a caduceus device, the traditional symbol of the Greek god Hermes composed of two snakes winding around a winged staff. Commensurate with his rank, his trousers have 1½in.-wide dark-blue welts in the outer seams.

(2) Medical surgeon with the rank of captain, 1861
Examining a soldier's medical-discharge document, this medical surgeon wears full dress. His Pattern 1858 hat has the brim looped up on the right side and fastened with a gold embroidered eagle insignia on a black velvet ground attached to its crown. Black ostrich feathers are attached on the left side and secured via a small "General Staff" button in a small black silk cockade. The hat has a gold embroidered wreath (**2a**) in front, on a black velvet ground, encircling the letters "MS" in silver, in Old English script, and a black and gold silk hat cord. All buttons on his officer's frock coat are "General Staff" pattern. Rank is indicated via shoulder straps with a dark-blue ground and gold embroidered border with two gold bars at each end. His dark-blue trousers have a ⅛in.-wide gold cord welt on the outer seams. He carries an ornate Model 1840 medical staff sword with the letters "MS" in Old English script on its guard. An emerald-green silk net waist sash with silk bullion fringe ends is worn under a Pattern 1861 sword belt with a Model 1851 brass belt plate.

(3) Private, Ambulance Corps, 1864
Holding a Halstead litter, or stretcher, this private assigned to the Ambulance Corps has a 1¼in. broad green band around his Pattern 1861 forage cap. His flannel sack coat is fastened by four large "General Service" buttons, and has a plain green worsted half-chevron attached above the elbow on each sleeve. He wears the plain sky-blue Pattern 1861 dismounted service trousers. He is armed with a Colt Navy revolver in a black leather holster on his Pattern 1839 waist belt, which has an oval "US" plate, and also carries an Allegheny Arsenal cap pouch and pistol cartridge box with a plain outer flap.

G: CORPS OF ENGINEERS AND ORDNANCE DEPARTMENT

(1) First lieutenant, Corps of Engineers, 1863
Using a theodolite, or "Transit" as it was called in the Civil War, this Corps of Engineers officer wears a Pattern 1858 forage cap with insignia (**1a**) at the front composed of a small "turreted castle" within a wreath on a dark-blue velvet ground. Its black leather chinstrap has a small "eagle and essayons" button at each end. His Pattern 1851 frock coat has nine large "eagle and essayons" buttons (**1b**) at the front, three small buttons of the same pattern on each cuff, and four large buttons of the same pattern on the pockets in the rear skirt. His dark-blue trousers have a ⅛in.-wide gold cord welt on the

outer seams. He has a Model 1850 staff officer's sword, with gold bullion sword knot, in a brass-mounted black leather scabbard.

(2) Private, Sappers, Miners, and Pontoniers, 1861

Uniformed as the Company of Sappers, Miners, and Pontoniers were when ordered to Washington, DC, in January 1861, this private wears a Pattern 1858 forage cap with rain cover. His plain cadet-gray jacket has nine "General Service" buttons at the front and plain cuffs. He wears plain dark-blue dismounted service trousers. He is armed with a US Model 1841 rifle, altered to .58 caliber. His accouterments consist of a Sapper and Miner-pattern belt with a two-piece "US" buckle, to which is attached a Model 1855 rifle cartridge box, Pattern 1850 black leather percussion-cap pouch, and black leather bayonet scabbard in leather frog carrying a saber bayonet with a solid brass hilt and crossguard. A Pattern 1858 canteen with brown jean wool cover is worn suspended from his right shoulder via a cloth strap, and his haversack is of black-painted canvas.

(3) Ordnance sergeant, 1864

Inspecting a saber bayonet, this ordnance sergeant wears a Pattern 1861 forage cap with a stamped-brass "flaming bomb" insignia at the front, and a small "General Service" button at either end of the black leather chinstrap. His dark-blue Pattern 1851 frock coat is trimmed with crimson on the collar and cuffs, with crimson silk sleeve insignia consisting of a five-pointed star above three point-down chevrons. He also has three diagonal crimson silk service stripes on each lower sleeve. All buttons have a "garter" inscribed "ORDNANCE CORPS" superimposed over crossed cannon barrels. His sky-blue kersey trousers have a 1½in.-wide scarlet welt on the outer seams. He carries a Model 1840 NCO sword with brass hilt and knuckle bow in a black leather scabbard with brass fittings, suspended via a sliding black leather frog from a Pattern 1851 waist belt with a rectangular "eagle" plate. Underneath his belt is a red worsted sash denoting his rank.

H: MILITARY TELEGRAPH SERVICE AND SIGNAL CORPS

(1) Telegrapher, Department of the Tennessee, 1864

Operating a Beardslee Magneto Dial Receiver, this military telegrapher wears a dark-blue Pattern 1861 forage cap with ⅛in.-wide silver cord around the top of its band. Worn over a collarless pullover shirt with four bone button placket front, his dark-blue vest has nine small "General Service" buttons down its front, and an off-white silk back with a brass buckle on an adjustable tie. His dark-blue enlisted man's mounted service trousers have a ⅛in.-wide silver welt on the outer seams. His brown leather calf-length boots with spurs attached are compatible with the mounted role performed by the Signal Corps.

(2) Second lieutenant, Signal Corps, 1864

Peering through a pair of French-made binoculars at a distant signal station, this Signal Corps officer wears a chasseur-pattern forage cap with a Signal Corps cloth embroidered patch at the front consisting of a white flag with red center square and a red flag with white center square, and gold embroidery for flagstaffs and border. A small "General Service" button is at each end of the chinstrap. His long officer-pattern sack coat has four "General Service" buttons at the front, a folded-down collar, and plain round cuffs. Rank is indicated by narrow solid gold braid and bullion shoulder straps. He has a dark-blue vest with a low-standing collar and

The taller soldier wears the sky-blue kersey uniform prescribed for the Invalid Corps on May 15, 1863. The sergeant accompanying him may also have been a member of the Invalid Corps, having been issued with a dark-blue frock coat. He has a folded talma, or rubberized poncho, over his left shoulder, and is holding a saber with scabbard attached to a white buff leather belt that has been reversed to compensate for the mirror image effect of the ambrotype. A mounted service weapon, the saber and accompanying accouterment is most likely a photographer's prop. (Daniel J. Binder collection)

nine small "General Service" buttons at the front, and his dark-blue trousers have ⅛in.-wide sky-blue welts on the outer seams. His brown leather calf-length boots have spurs attached. He carries a privately purchased officer's leather haversack with leather shoulder straps and a Bartholomae Patent Filter Canteen with brown wool cover, suspended from a leather strap with roller buckle.

(3) Private, Signal Corps, 1864

Holding small canvas signal disks and relaying a field signal, this Signal Corps private carries over his shoulder equipment consisting of a copper fuel canteen, plus a signal light box and canvas haversack containing night-signaling equipment. He wears a civilian felt "pork-pie" hat with gray worsted cord. His mounted service jacket has 11 small "General Service" buttons down its front and two buttons of the same size and pattern on each cuff. On the sleeve of his jacket is displayed a Signal Corps patch (3a) consisting of red-and-white "crossed flags" on a dark-blue cloth ground. He wears plain sky-blue kersey mounted service trousers and black leather boots with spurs.

INDEX